Anders Lu

If You Don't Let Us Dream,
We Won't Let You Sleep

Methuen Drama

Bloomsbury Methuen Drama

An imprint of Bloomsbury Publishing Plc

50 Bedford Square
London
WC1B 3DP
UK

175 Fifth Avenue
New York
NY 10010
USA

www.bloomsbury.com

First published 2013

A catalogue record for this book is available from the British Library

ISBN
PB: 978-1-4725-1357-1
ePub: 978-1-4725-0942-0

Typeset by Country Setting, Kingsdown, Kent CT14 8ES
Printed and bound in Great Britain

ROYAL COURT

The Royal Court Theatre presents

IF YOU DON'T LET US DREAM, WE WON'T LET YOU SLEEP

by **Anders Lustgarten**

IF YOU DON'T LET US DREAM, WE WON'T LET YOU SLEEP was first performed at The Royal Court Jerwood Theatre Downstairs, Sloane Square, on Friday 15th February 2013.

IF YOU DON'T LET US DREAM, WE WON'T LET YOU SLEEP is part of the Royal Court's Jerwood New Playwrights programme, supported by the Jerwood Charitable Foundation.

IF YOU DON'T LET US DREAM, WE WON'T LET YOU SLEEP

by Anders Lustgarten

Cast in alphabetical order
Joan **Susan Brown**
Thacker/Thomas/Ross **Ben Dilloway**
Kelly/Nurse/Teacher 2/Lucinda **Laura Elphinstone**
Ryan **Daniel Kendrick**
Workman/Jason/Ray **Damien Molony**
Taylor/McDonald Moyo **Lucian Msamati**
James Asset-Smith/Zebedee **Ferdy Roberts**
Administrator/Teacher 1/Karen McLean/Jen **Meera Syal**
All other parts played by members of the company

Director **Simon Godwin**
Design Consultant **Lucy Sierra**
Lighting Designer **Jack Williams**
Sound Designer **David McSeveney**
Casting Director **Amy Ball**
Assistant Director **Ned Bennett**
Associate Sound Designer **Joel Price**
Production Manager **Tariq Rifaat**
Stage Manager **Michael Dennis**
Deputy Stage Manager **Pippa Meyer**
Assistant Stage Manager **Ralph Buchanan**
Stage Management Work Placement **Heather Cryan**
Costume Supervisor **Jackie Orton**

The Royal Court & Stage Management wish to thank the following for their help with this production:
Lucian Msamati & Denton Chikura for Shona translation, Atlantic Blanket Company,
What More UK Ltd, Chelsea Scaffolding, Keir Bosley.

THE COMPANY

ANDERS LUSTGARTEN (Writer)

THEATRE INCLUDES: Socialism is Great (National Theatre Connections); Theatre Uncut (Theatre Uncut/Traverse); Capitalism: A Lecture Series (Lyric Hammersmith); A Day at the Racists, The Insurgents, Enduring Freedom (Finborough); Black Jesus (Harare International Theatre Festival); A Torture Comedy (Actors Centre); The Police (BAC); The Punishment Stories (Soho/Hampstead).

RADIO INCLUDES: No.10: Democracy in Traction, The Hamster.

Anders was the inaugural winner of the Harold Pinter Playwright's Award and won the Catherine Johnson Award in 2011 for A Day at the Racists. Anders is also an international political activist who is currently working to stop so-called development banks privatising North Africa.

NED BENNETT (Assistant Director)

AS ASSISTANT DIRECTOR FOR THE ROYAL COURT: No Quarter.

AS DIRECTOR, OTHER THEATRE INCLUDES: Mercury Fur (Old Red Lion/Trafalgar Studios); Mr Noodles (Royal Exchange, Manchester); Blue Rabbits (Templeworks); Excellent Choice (Old Vic Tunnels); A Butcher of Distinction (King's Head); Edmond (Theatre Royal, Haymarket); Smartcard (Shunt Vaults); Selling Clive (Lost).

AS ASSISTANT DIRECTOR, OTHER THEATRE INCLUDES: Of Mice & Men (Watermill); A Letter to England (Finborough); Odette (Bridewell); Vent (Contact).

SUSAN BROWN (Joan)

FOR THE ROYAL COURT: Goodbye to All That, Road, Shirley, Downfall, Gibraltar Strait, Seagulls.

OTHER THEATRE INCLUDES: Harper Regan, The Hour We Knew Nothing of Each Other, Playing With Fire, Henry IV Parts I & II, Cardiff East (National); Easter, Romeo & Juliet, Richard III, Bad Weather (RSC); Saved (Lyric Hammersmith); Dying For It, Butterfly Kiss (Almeida); Making Noise Quietly, The Wild Duck (Donmar); The Contingency Plan (Bush); The Chairs, The House of Bernarda Alba (Gate); You Be Ted & I'll Be Sylvia (Hampstead); The Beaux' Stratagem, Back to Methuselah, The Vortex, The Way of the World, A Woman of No Importance (Cambridge Theatre Company); Playing Sinatra (Warehouse/Greenwich Theatre); Small Change, Iphigenia (Sheffield Theatres).

TELEVISION INCLUDES: Call the Midwife, Broadchurch, Stella, Midsomer Murders, Waking the Dead, Game of Thrones, Torchwood, Silent Witness, Blue Dove, Dalziel & Pascoe, Brides in the Bath, La Femme Musketeer, Rose & Maloney, Pinochet in Suburbia, Loving Hazel, Making Out, Coronation Street, Absolute Hell, Nona, Prime Suspect, The Riff Raff Element, September Song, A Touch of Frost, Taggart, Wokenwell, Anorak of Fire, The Vice, Wire in the Blood, The Best of Both Worlds, Road.

FILM INCLUDES: Belle, The Iron Lady, Now Is Good, Brideshead Revisited, Hope & Glory.

BEN DILLOWAY (Thacker/Thomas/Ross)

THEATRE INCLUDES: King Lear (Almeida); Mercury Fur, Step 9 (of 12) (Trafalgar Studios); Footpath (High Tide); Mercury Fur (The Old Red Lion); Excellent Choice (Vault: The Old Vic Tunnels); Underground (503); Angry Young Man (Arcola); Chicken (Southwark Playhouse); Tape (Counter Culture); But Otherwise Went Well (Waterloo East); Orphans (Lindbury Studio); The 24 Hour Plays (Old Vic).

FILM INCLUDES: Jess//Jim, Hold On Me, The Archer.

LAURA ELPHINSTONE (Kelly/ Nurse/Teacher 2/Lucinda)

FOR THE ROYAL COURT: Love & Information, Breathing Corpses, Country Music.

OTHER THEATRE INCLUDES: Utopia (Soho/Live, Newcastle); Chalet Lines (Bush); Top Girls (Chichester/Trafalgar Studios); A Month In The Country (Chichester); Marine Parade (Brighton Festival); Pains Of Youth, Women Of Troy (National); Bedroom Farce (West Yorkshire Playhouse); Far From The Madding Crowd (ETT tour); Glass Eels (Hampstead); Heatbreak House (Watford Palace); Scenes From An Execution (Hackney Empire); Tom & Viv (Almeida); The Crucible (RSC/West End); Pictures of Clay (Royal Exchange).

TELEVISION INCLUDES: Holby, Doctors, My So Called Life Sentence, Tess Of The D'Urberbilles.

FILM INCLUDES: Leave to Remain, The History Boys.

RADIO INCLUDES: The Final Count, Interviews, Hard Road, Cooking With Stanley.

SIMON GODWIN (Director)

FOR THE ROYAL COURT: NSFW, The Witness, Goodbye to All That, The Acid Test, Pagans (International Playwrights Season 2011), Wanderlust, Hung Over: Ten Short Plays About The Election (Rough Cut), Black Beast Sadness (Off the Wall Season Reading), Hassan Lekliche (I Come From There Season Reading).

OTHER THEATRE INCLUDES: Krapp's Last Tape/A Kind Of Alaska, Faith Healer, Far Away (Bristol Old Vic); The Winter's Tale (Headlong with Nuffield Theatre & Schtanhaus/UK tour); All the Little Things We Crushed (Almeida Projects); The Country (Tabard); The Seagull, Habeas Corpus, Relatively Speaking (Royal & Derngate Theatres, Northampton); Quartermaine's Terms (Royal & Derngate Theatres/Salisbury Playhouse); Mister Heracles (West Yorkshire Playhouse); Romeo & Juliet (Cambridge Arts); All's Well That Ends Well (Straydogs/UK tour); Eurydice (Straydogs, BAC/Trafalgar Studios).

OPERA INCLUDES: Inkle & Yarico (Straydogs).

Simon is co-founder of Straydogs Theatre Company and is currently an Associate Director of Bristol Old Vic and the Royal Court.

DANIEL KENDRICK (Ryan)

FOR THE ROYAL COURT: Ding Dong the Wicked, Vera Vera Vera.

OTHER THEATRE INCLUDES: Rosie & Jim (Mobculture); Chapel Street (Liverpool Playhouse/Old Red Lion); Coalition (503).

TELEVISION INCLUDES: Run, Eastenders, 999.

FILM INCLUDES: Offender, Lovebite.

DAVID McSEVENEY (Sound Designer)

FOR THE ROYAL COURT: Constellations (& West End), Vera Vera Vera, The Village Bike, Clybourne Park (& West End), Ingredient X, Posh, Disconnect, Cock, A Miracle, The Stone, Shades, 7 Jewish Children, The Girlfriend Experience (& Theatre Royal Plymouth/Young Vic), Contractions, Fear & Misery/War & Peace.

OTHER THEATRE INCLUDES: The Tin Horizon (503); Gaslight (Old Vic); Charley's Aunt, An Hour & a Half Late (Theatre Royal, Bath); A Passage to India, After Mrs Rochester, Madame Bovary (Shared Experience); Men Should Weep, Rookery Nook (Oxford Stage Company); Othello (Southwark Playhouse).

AS ASSISTANT DESIGNER: The Permanent Way (Out of Joint); My Brilliant Divorce, Auntie & Me (West End); Accidental Death of an Anarchist (Donmar).

David is Head of Sound at the Royal Court.

DAMIEN MOLONY (Workman/Jason/Ray)

THEATRE INCLUDES: Travelling Light (National); 'Tis Pity She's a Whore (West Yorkshire Playhouse).

TELEVISION INCLUDES: Being Human.

RADIO INCLUDES: The Hill Bachelors, Carrel 16 - Fifth Floor - Ussher Library.

LUCIAN MSAMATI (Taylor/McDonald Moyo)

FOR THE ROYAL COURT: Belong (with Tiata Fahodzi), Clybourne Park (& West End).

THEATRE INCLUDES: Comedy of Errors, Death & the King's Horseman, The Overwhelming, President of an Empty Room, Mourning Becomes Electra (National); Ruined, ID (Almeida); The Resistable Rise of Arturo Ui, The Firework-Maker's Daughter (Lyric Hammersmith); 1807 – The First Act (Globe); Pericles (RSC); Fabulation, Gem of the Ocean, Walk Hard (Tricycle); Who Killed Mr Drum? (Riverside Studios); Romeo & Juliet (Dancehouse, Manchester); The Taming of the Shrew (& director – Bath Shakespeare Festival); Born African (Arthur Seaton, New York); Twelfth Night (Neuss Globe, Germany); Fade to Black (Harare International Festival of Arts); Eternal Peace Asylum (Over the Edge/American Repertory); The Rocky Horror Picture Show (Seven Arts).

TELEVISION INCLUDES: Game of Thrones, Death in Paradise, Richard II, Ashes to Ashes, Doctor Who, The No. 1 Ladies' Detective Agency, The Andi O Show, Spooks, Ultimate Force, Too Close for Comfort, The Knock.

FILM INCLUDES: The International, Dr Juju, Lumumba.

RADIO INCLUDES: The Jero Plays, Colours, The Mugabe Plays, Seventh Street Alchemy.

AWARDS INCLUDE: Award for Outstanding Creative Contribution to Radio, Creative Directors' Forum of Zimbabwe.

Lucian has also worked extensively as a radio producer and presenter, playwright, copywriter and director for stage, screen and audio recording. He is the Artistic Director of Tiata Fahodzi.

FERDY ROBERTS (James Asset-Smith/Zebedee)

FOR THE ROYAL COURT: Playing the Victim (with Told By An Idiot).

OTHER THEATRE INCLUDES: Three Kingdoms (Lyric Hammersmith/No.99 Estonia/Munich Kammerspiele); Three Sisters (Filter/Lyric Hammersmith); A Midsummer Night's Dream (Filter/Lyric Hammersmith/Royal Exchange, Manchester); Silence (Filter/RSC); Water (Filter/Lyric Hammersmith/Sydney Theatre Company/tour); Wallenstein, The Sea (Chichester); Twelfth Night (Filter/Tricycle/RSC/international tour); On Religion (Théatre de Poche, Brussels); Caucasian Chalk Circle (National/Filter/tour); The Birthday Party, The Dumb Waiter, Aladdin (Bristol Old Vic); Girl in a Goldfish Bowl (Crucible Studio); Frankenstein (Derby Playhouse); Switchback (Tron/Sweetscar); Faster (Filter/international tour); The Contractor (Oxford Stage Company); Another Company (West End); The Rise & Fall of Little Voice, The Changling, Beautiful Thing (Salisbury Playhouse); Ghosts (Alhambra Studio).

TELEVISION INCLUDES: MI High, Whistleblower, The Bill, Goldplated, Your Mother Should Know, Holby City, Doctors, A Touch of Frost.

FILM INCLUDES: What You Will, Mr Nice, Sex & Drugs & Rock & Roll, Honest.

Ferdy is Co-Artistic Director of Filter Theatre and an Associate Artist at Lyric Theatre Hammersmith.

LUCY SIERRA (Design Consultant)

FOR THE ROYAL COURT, AS ASSOCIATE DESIGNER: In the Republic of Happiness.

FOR THE ROYAL COURT, AS ASSISTANT DESIGNER: Love & Information, Cock, Get Santa!, Sucker Punch.

AS DESIGNER, OTHER THEATRE INCLUDES: Symmetry (Southwark Playhouse); Sweeney Todd, David Copperfield, White Nights (Octagon, Bolton); Earthquakes in London (as associate – National/Headlong); Songs Inside (Gate/ATC); The Nose (Shared Property/tour); The Guests (Etcetera); Grimethorpe Race, Dry Lightning (Arcola); Fewer Emergencies (Burton Taylor at Oxford Playhouse); Cahoots Macbeth (Southwark Playhouse/PEN International Festival), The Tempest, Shakespeare & Sibelius (BBC/Barbican); Into The Woods (Greenwich); Blue Funk (Old Red Lion).

AS ASSISTANT DESIGNER, OTHER THEATRE INCLUDES: The Effect (National), Wild Swans, Government Inspector (Young Vic), Carmen (Salzburg Festspielhaus).

MEERA SYAL (Administrator/Teacher 1/Karen McLean/Jen)

FOR THE ROYAL COURT: The Great Celestial Cow (& tour), Minor Complications, True Dare Kiss, Byrthrite, Serious Money (& West End/The Public Theatre, NYC).

OTHER THEATRE INCLUDES: Much Ado About Nothing (RSC); The Killing of Sister George (Arts Theatre); Shirley Valentine (Menier Chocolate Factory/Trafalgar Studios); Rafta, Rafta, Peer Gynt (National); Bombay Dreams (Really Useful Theatre Company); The Vagina Monologues (Old Vic/Ambassadors/Madison Square Gardens, NYC); One of Us (Edinburgh Festival Fringe/Soho); Kissing God (Hampstead); All the Fun of the Fair (Half Moon); The Oppressed Minorities Big Fun Show (& Edinburgh Festival Fringe); School for Scandal (Bristol Old Vic); Kirti Sona & Ba (Leicester Haymarket); My Girl (Theatre Royal, Stratford East); 24 Hour Plays & 24 Hour Musicals (Old Vic).

TELEVISION INCLUDES: Nemesis, Family Tree, The Jury, Doctor Who, Little Crackers, Holby City, Minder, Beautiful People, Jekyll, The Amazing Mrs Pritchard, The Secretary Who Stole £4 Million, Life Isn't All Ha Ha Hee Hee, Who Do You Think You Are?, Linda Green, The Kumars at No. 42, Fat Friends, The Agency, Forgive & Forget, Mrs Bradley Mysteries, Goodness Gracious Me, Absolutely Fabulous, Sean's Show, The Jo Brand Show, My Sister Wife, Taggart, Kinsey, The Bureaucracy of Love, Majdhar, To Have & To Hold, A Little Princess, The Secret Diary of Adrian Mole, The Real McCoy, Have I Got News For You, Soldier, Soldier, Crossing the Floor, Holding On, Drop the Dead Donkey.

FILM INCLUDES: All in Good Time, You Will Meet a Tall Dark Stranger, Desert Flower, Mad, Sad & Bad, Jhoom Barabar Jhoom, Scoop, Anita & Me, Beautiful Thing, A Nice Arrangement, Sammi & Rosie Get Laid, It's Not Unusual.

RADIO INCLUDES: A Small Town Murder, Everyday Tales of Afghan Folk, Pather Panchali, Duty Free, Leaving Normal, Prisoner 1084, Kipling in Love, Ladies Excuse Me, Women's Troubles…, Wicked Words, Morning Story, Pankhiraj, World Service, Goodness Gracious Me.

AWARDS INCLUDE: Women In Film & TV Creative Originality Award; Two British Comedy Awards (Goodness Gracious Me, The Kumars at No. 42); Two International Emmys (The Kumars at No. 42); WhatsOnStage.com Award for Best Solo Performance (Shirley Valentine).

JACK WILLIAMS (Lighting Designer)

AS LIGHTING DESIGNER, FOR THE ROYAL COURT: Ding Dong The Wicked.

AS RE-LIGHTER, FOR THE ROYAL COURT: Vera Vera Vera.

AS LIGHTING DESIGNER, THEATRE INCLUDES: Cowardy Custard, Les Misérables (Canterbury Marlowe); The Storm, The Killing Game (BAC); Book Of Little Things (Oval House).

AS ASSOCIATE LIGHTING DESIGNER, THEATRE INCLUDES: Ragtime, A Midsummer's Night Dream (Regent's Park).

AS PRODUCTION LX/RE-LIGHTER, OTHER THEATRE INCLUDES: Scrooge: The Musical, Half a Sixpence (UK tours); Joseph & the Amazing Technicolor Dreamcoat (Japan); Opera Holland Park; La Cage Aux Folles (Playhouse); Dreamboats & Petticoats (Savoy/Playhouse/UK tour); Swallows & Amazons (Vaudeville); Plague Over England (The Duchess); Pleasance 2007-2011 (Edinburgh).

AS ASSISTANT LIGHTING DESIGNER, OPERA INCLUDES: The Magic Flute, Albert Herring (British Youth Opera).

AS PRODUCTION LX, OPERA INCLUDES: Don Pasquale, L'Amico Fritz (Opera Holland Park).

Jack is Head of Lighting at the Royal Court Theatre.

JERWOOD CHARITABLE FOUNDATION

Jerwood New Playwrights is a longstanding partnership between the Jerwood Charitable Foundation and the Royal Court. Each year, Jerwood New Playwrights supports the production of three new works by emerging writers, all of whom are in the first 10 years of their career.

The Royal Court carefully identifies playwrights whose careers would benefit from the challenge and profile of being fully produced either in the Jerwood Downstairs or Jerwood Upstairs Theatres at the Royal Court.

The programme has produced a collection of challenging and outspoken works which explore a variety of new forms and voices and so far has supported the production of 74 new plays.

These plays include: Anya Reiss' SPUR OF THE MOMENT and THE ACID TEST, Penelope Skinner's THE VILLAGE BIKE, Rachel De-lahay's THE WESTBRIDGE, Joe Penhall's SOME VOICES, Mark Ravenhill's SHOPPING AND FUCKING (co-production with Out of Joint), Ayub Khan Din's EAST IS EAST (co-production with Tamasha), Martin McDonagh's THE BEAUTY QUEEN OF LEENANE (co-production with Druid Theatre Company), Conor McPherson's THE WEIR, Nick Grosso's REAL CLASSY AFFAIR, Sarah Kane's 4.48 PSYCHOSIS, Gary Mitchell's THE FORCE OF CHANGE, David Eldridge's UNDER THE BLUE SKY, David Harrower's PRESENCE, Simon Stephens' HERONS, Roy Williams' CLUBLAND, Leo Butler's REDUNDANT, Michael Wynne's THE PEOPLE ARE FRIENDLY, David Greig's OUTLYING ISLANDS, Zinnie Harris' NIGHTINGALE AND CHASE, Grae Cleugh's FUCKING GAMES, Rona Munro's IRON, Richard Bean's UNDER THE WHALEBACK, Ché Walker's FLESH WOUND, Roy Williams' FALLOUT, Mick Mahoney's FOOD CHAIN, Ayub Khan Din's NOTES ON FALLING LEAVES, Leo Butler's LUCKY DOG, Simon Stephens' COUNTRY MUSIC, Laura Wade's BREATHING CORPSES, Debbie Tucker Green's STONING MARY, David Eldridge's INCOMPLETE AND RANDOM ACTS OF KINDNESS, Gregory Burke's ON TOUR, Stella Feehily's O GO MY MAN, Simon Stephens' MOTORTOWN, Simon Farquhar's RAINBOW KISS, April de Angelis, Stella Feehily, Tanika Gupta, Chloe Moss and Laura Wade's CATCH, Mike Bartlett's MY CHILD, Polly Stenham's THAT FACE, Alexi Kaye Campbell's THE PRIDE, Fiona Evans' SCARBOROUGH, Levi David Addai's OXFORD STREET, Bola Agbaje's GONE TOO FAR!, Alia Bano's SHADES, Polly Stenham's TUSK TUSK, Tim Crouch's THE AUTHOR, Bola Agbaje's OFF THE ENDZ and DC Moore's THE EMPIRE.

In 2012, Jerwood New Playwrights supported Nick Payne's CONSTELLATIONS, Vivienne Franzmann's THE WITNESS and E.V.Crowe's HERO.

The Jerwood Charitable Foundation is dedicated to imaginative and responsible revenue funding of the arts, supporting artists to develop and grow at important stages in their careers. It works with artists across art forms, from dance and theatre to literature, music and the visual arts. www.jerwoodcharitablefoundation.org.

THE ENGLISH STAGE COMPANY
AT THE ROYAL COURT THEATRE

'For me the theatre is really a religion or way of life. You must decide what you feel the world is about and what you want to say about it, so that everything in the theatre you work in is saying the same thing ... A theatre must have a recognisable attitude. It will have one, whether you like it or not.'

George Devine, first artistic director of the English Stage Company: notes for an unwritten book.

photo: Stephen Cummiskey

As Britain's leading national company dedicated to new work, the Royal Court Theatre produces new plays of the highest quality, working with writers from all backgrounds, and addressing the problems and possibilities of our time.

"The Royal Court has been at the centre of British cultural life for the past 50 years, an engine room for new writing and constantly transforming the theatrical culture." Stephen Daldry

Since its foundation in 1956, the Royal Court has presented premieres by almost every leading contemporary British playwright, from John Osborne's Look Back in Anger to Caryl Churchill's A Number and Tom Stoppard's Rock 'n' Roll. Just some of the other writers to have chosen the Royal Court to premiere their work include Edward Albee, John Arden, Richard Bean, Samuel Beckett, Edward Bond, Leo Butler, Jez Butterworth, Martin Crimp, Ariel Dorfman, Stella Feehily, Christopher Hampton, David Hare, Eugène Ionesco, Ann Jellicoe, Terry Johnson, Sarah Kane, David Mamet, Martin McDonagh, Conor McPherson, Joe Penhall, Lucy Prebble, Mark Ravenhill, Simon Stephens, Wole Soyinka, Polly Stenham, David Storey, Debbie Tucker Green, Arnold Wesker and Roy Williams.

"It is risky to miss a production there." Financial Times

In addition to its full-scale productions, the Royal Court also facilitates international work at a grass roots level, developing exchanges which bring young writers to Britain and sending British writers, actors and directors to work with artists around the world. The research and play development arm of the Royal Court Theatre, The Studio, finds the most exciting and diverse range of new voices in the UK. The Studio runs play-writing groups including the Young Writers Programme, Critical Mass for black, Asian and minority ethnic writers and the biennial Young Writers Festival. For further information, go to www.royalcourttheatre.com/playwriting/the-studio.

"Yes, the Royal Court is on a roll. Yes, Dominic Cooke has just the genius and kick that this venue needs... It's fist-bitingly exciting." Independent

Spring 2013

ROYAL COURT

Jerwood Theatre Downstairs

21 Mar– 11 May 2013

the low road
by Bruce Norris

A fable of free market economics and cut-throat capitalism.
Bruce Norris' previous plays include *Clybourne Park* at the Royal Court.

Jerwood Theatre Upstairs

22 Feb–23 Mar 2013

a time to reap
by Anna Wakulik, translated by Catherine Grosvenor

An exciting new voice looking at Poland's hottest
political topics – abortion and the Catholic Church.
International Playwrights: A Genesis Foundation Project

5 Apr–4 May 2013

a new play
written and directed by Anthony Neilson

Neilson is renowned for his ground-breaking and imaginative new work.

Royal Court Theatre and Fuel co-production
11 May–8 Jun 2013

the victorian in the wall
by Will Adamsdale

Perrier Award-winning Adamsdale's new play contains jokes, songs, banging
on recycling boxes and a talking fridge…

020 7565 5000
www.royalcourttheatre.com

Sloane Square ⇄ Victoria 🅱 royalcourt 🅵 theroyalcourttheatre

Supported using public funding by
**ARTS COUNCIL
ENGLAND**

ROYAL COURT SUPPORTERS

The Royal Court has significant and longstanding relationships with many organisations and individuals who provide vital support. It is this support that makes possible its unique playwriting and audience development programmes.

Coutts is the Principal Sponsor of the Royal Court. The Genesis Foundation supports the Royal Court's work with International Playwrights. Theatre Local is sponsored by Bloomberg. The Jerwood Charitable Foundation supports new plays by playwrights through the Jerwood New Playwrights series. The Andrew Lloyd Webber Foundation supports the Royal Court's Studio, which aims to seek out, nurture and support emerging playwrights.

The Harold Pinter Playwright's Award is given annually by his widow, Lady Antonia Fraser, to support a new commission at the Royal Court.

PUBLIC FUNDING
Arts Council England, London
British Council
European Commission Representation in the UK

CHARITABLE DONATIONS
Martin Bowley Charitable Trust
Columbia Foundation Fund of the London
Community Foundation
Cowley Charitable Trust
The Dorset Foundation
The John Ellerman Foundation
The Eranda Foundation
Genesis Foundation
J Paul Getty Jnr Charitable Trust
The Golden Bottle Trust
The Haberdashers' Company
Jerwood Charitable Foundation
Marina Kleinwort Trust
The Andrew Lloyd Webber Foundation
John Lyon's Charity
The Andrew W. Mellon Foundation
Rose Foundation
The Royal College of Psychiatrists
Royal Victoria Hall Foundation
The Dr Mortimer & Theresa Sackler Foundation
John Thaw Foundation
The Vandervell Foundation
The Garfield Weston Foundation

CORPORATE SUPPORTERS & SPONSORS
BBC
Bloomberg
Coutts
Ecosse Films
Kudos Film & Television
MAC
Moët & Chandon
Oakley Capital Limited
Smythson of Bond Street
White Light Ltd

BUSINESS ASSOCIATES, MEMBERS & BENEFACTORS
Annoushka
Auerbach & Steele Opticians
Bank of America Merrill Lynch
Byfield Consultancy
Hugo Boss
Lazard
Savills
Troy Asset Management
Vanity Fair

DEVELOPMENT ADVOCATES
John Ayton MBE
Elizabeth Bandeen
Kinvara Balfour
Anthony Burton CBE
Piers Butler
Sindy Caplan
Sarah Chappatte
Cas Donald (Vice Chair)
Celeste Fenichel
Emma Marsh (Chair)
Deborah Shaw Marquardt (Vice Chair)
Tom Siebens
Sian Westerman
Nick Wheeler
Daniel Winterfeldt

Supported by
ARTS COUNCIL ENGLAND

INDIVIDUAL MEMBERS

GROUND-BREAKERS

Anonymous
Moira Andreae
Allen Appen & Jane Wiest
Mr & Mrs Simon Andrews
Nick Archdale
Charlotte Asprey
Jane Attias
Brian Balfour-Oatts
Elizabeth & Adam Bandeen
Ray Barrell & Ursula Van Almsick
Dr Kate Best
Sarah Blomfield
Stan & Val Bond
Kristina Borsy & Nick Turdean
Neil & Sarah Brener
Deborah Brett
Mrs Joanna Buckhenham
Lois Moore & Nigel Burridge
Louise Burton
Clive & Helena Butler
Sindy & Jonathan Caplan
Gavin & Lesley Casey
Sarah & Philippe Chappatte
Tim & Caroline Clark
Carole & Neville Conrad
Anthony & Andrea Coombs
Clyde Cooper
Ian & Caroline Cormack
Mr & Mrs Cross
Andrew & Amanda Cryer
Alison Davies
Matthew Dean
Roger & Alison De Haan
Noel De Keyzer
Polly Devlin OBE
Sophie Diedrichs-Cox
Glen Donovan
Denise & Randolph Dumas
Robyn Durie
Zeina Durra & Saadi Soudavar
Glenn & Phyllida Earle
The Edwin Fox Foundation
Mark & Sarah Evans
Margaret Exley CBE
Celeste & Peter Fenichel
Beverley Gee
Nick & Julie Gould
Lord & Lady Grabiner
Richard & Marcia Grand
Reade & Elizabeth Griffith
Don & Sue Guiney
Jill Hackel & Andrzej Zarzycki
Carol Hall
Jennifer & Stephen Harper
Sam & Caroline Haubold
Madeleine Hodgkin
Mr & Mrs Gordon Holmes
Damien Hyland
Susie & David Hyman
Amanda Ibbetson
Nicholas Jones
David Kaskel & Christopher Teano
Vincent & Amanda Keaveny
Peter & Maria Kellner
Nicola Kerr
Philip & Joan Kingsley
Mr & Mrs Pawel Kisielewski
Sarah & David Kowitz
Rosemary Leith
Larry & Peggy Levy
Imelda Liddiard
Daisy & Richard Littler
Kathryn Ludlow
Beatrice & James Lupton CBE
Dr Ekaterina Malievskaia & George Goldsmith
Christopher Marek Rencki
Andy McIver
Barbara Minto
Shafin & Angelie Moledina
Ann & Gavin Neath CBE
Clive & Annie Norton
Georgia Oetker
Mr & Mrs Sandy Orr
Mr & Mrs Guy Patterson
Sir William & Lady Vanessa Patey
William Plapinger & Cassie Murray
Andrea & Hilary Ponti
Lauren Prakke
Annie & Preben Prebensen
Mrs Ivetta Rabinovich
Julie Ritter
Mark & Tricia Robinson
Paul & Gill Robinson
Sir & Lady Ruddock
William & Hilary Russell
Julie & Bill Ryan
Sally & Anthony Salz
Bhags Sharma
J Sheridan
The Michael & Melanie Sherwood Charitable Foundation
Tom Siebens & Mimi Parsons
Andy Simpkin
Anthony Simpson & Susan Boster
Andrea Sinclair & Serge Kremer
Paul & Rita Skinner
Mr & Mrs RAH Smart
Brian Smith
Mr Michael Spencer
Sue St Johns
The Ulrich Family
The Ury Trust
Amanda Vail
Constanze Von Unruh
Ian & Victoria Watson & The Watson Foundation
Matthew & Sian Westerman
Anne-Marie Williams
Sir Robert & Lady Wilson
Daniel Winterfeldt & Jonathan Leonhart
Martin & Sally Woodcock
Kate & Michael Yates

BOUNDARY-BREAKERS

Anonymous
Katie Bradford
David Harding
Steve Kingshott
Emma Marsh
Philippa Thorp
Mr & Mrs Nick Wheeler

MOVER-SHAKERS

Eric Abraham
Anonymous
Christine Collins
Lloyd & Sarah Dorfman
Piers & Melanie Gibson
Lydia & Manfred Gorvy
Mr & Mrs Roderick Jack
Duncan Matthews QC
Ian & Carol Sellars
Nicholas Stanley
Edgar & Judith Wallner

MAJOR DONORS

Anonymous
Rob & Siri Cope
Cas Donald
Jack & Linda Keenan
Adam Kenwright
Miles Morland
NoraLee & Jon Sedmak
Jan & Michael Topham
Stuart & Hilary Williams Charitable Foundation

Thank you to all our Friends, Stage-Takers and Ice-Breakers for their generous support.

Introduction

So this is where I think we are, at the start of the second decade of the twenty-first century, on this fascinating and infuriating small wet island that firmly believes it's approximately 3,000 miles further west than it actually is:

AUSTERITY WAS NEVER ABOUT FIXING THE ECONOMY
Or we wouldn't be in triple dip recession. Not even Gideon Oliver Osborne, heir to the baronetcy of Ballentaylor and Ballylemon and thus the ideal embodiment of Tory attacks on 'entitlement culture', is that inept. Austerity is about fundamentally reshaping not just government but our basic understanding of what it means to be a member of society, in order to serve the needs of financial markets.

KILL THE ZOMBIE
The austerity boys get away with it because hardly anyone understands financial capitalism, but mainly due to a killer zombie. The 'market knows best' paradigm, born in the seventies amidst the uncollected rubbish of the three-day week, died in spectacular fashion in the 2008 banking collapse, which proved financial institutions to be as trustworthy and productive as one of their NINJA loans. But like in the George A. Romero films, the zombie won't die! In fact the zombipocalyptic idea of the infallible private sector is chomping away on ever more of the real economy and people's lives . . .

KEYNES IS DEAD
In large part because the zombie's traditional foe has expired too. The Keynesian idea of the state as the moral and economic alternative to the private sector, which animated the Left for most of the twentieth century (not the Blairite 'left', obviously, which was animated by non-executive directorships and black cod miso) looks far gone when the private sector now runs the state and soaks it for bailouts and subsidies.
All political parties cringe before the market. The result is that, in an era that touts 'choice' as its cardinal virtue, politically we have none.

POST-PARTY POLITICS

And yet in a way that's great – we're starting to leave the old corrupted dichotomy of Labour and Tory behind, and look for new forms of political engagement. The political lesson of the twentieth century is that concentrated power, whether fascist, corporate or vanguard of the proletariat, produces catastrophes. So the question for the twenty-first century is what shape our new political forms will take. The most immediately exciting stuff is grassroots action, of which Occupy was one type and the riots another.

RADICAL OPTIMISM

What turns people off conventional politics is a sense that it won't make a difference, and direct action gives you that feeling of making a difference back. It also gives you a sense of optimism and excitement, and optimism is about the most radical quality you can possess right now. But on its own, can grassroots action control financial flows? Can it reconfigure institutions and structures to serve people instead of speculative capital? Unlikely. So our paradoxical relationship to institutions of power, who only listen to us when we make it clear we reject them, is what we need to think about next.

So that's the intellectual chain of thought that made me write this play. But it's only one part of why I wrote it.

I wrote it because a few years ago I was teaching in prison, and my friend Esther Baker put on a version of *Accidental Death of an Anarchist*, which I rewrote to be about the Stephen Lawrence case. Prisoners are a loud group of people and not easily inclined to silence, but (apart from the bits where we had to physically remove large men from the stage as they argued with the characters about various plot twists) they were spellbound. That was my first real experience of the theatre, and of the joy of storytelling in particular.

I wrote it because I love the feeling in a room of an audience and a cast feeling and creating something collectively. It's a microcosm of a good society.

I wrote it because at its heart this system of finance that now dominates us is quite simple under its impossibly convoluted technicalities, and I want to help people understand it. What they do with that knowledge is up to them.

I wrote it because now's the time for the return of proper political theatre. Not old-style agitprop, but 'anti-prop' that takes on the overwhelming reality of 2013: the propaganda of markets that they're indispensible. What if we put up taxes and the bankers threatened to leave? Well, (a) they wouldn't, because there's nowhere else with such lax regulatory and tax regimes, where their kids can be poshly educated and they speak English and have Michelin-starred restaurants and nobody bothers you. The people who love London the most are the twenty-year-old Italian kid escaping Mama and the fifty-year-old hedge-fund manager escaping tax, both for the same reason: nobody's watching them. But (b), we'd be much better off, because we wouldn't be paying trillions in bailouts, because our whole society wouldn't be under the sway of a tiny interest group, and because we are capable, talented people who'd find more productive ways to make a living. You want to leave? Enjoy Russia. Say hi to Gerard Depardieu and tell him I burnt every DVD of *Cyrano de Bergerac* I could lay my hands on.

I wrote it to make you feel, and therefore to think. Hope it worked.

Anders Lustgarten,
January 2013

Acknowledgements

It takes a lot of people to write a good play. Laurence Lustgarten, Donna Dickenson and Chris Britton got me to adulthood (more or less). Esther Baker and Simon Stephens got me into theatre. Nick Hildyard is a political inspiration. Angela Debnath a personal one. Joseph Rochlitz provided a place to write. Neil McPherson took the first theatrical chance on me. Chris Campbell and Dominic Cooke took the biggest one. There are dozens of people who've made this play possible in some way, but I'll go all Gwyneth Paltrow if I list all of you. Thank you.

This play is dedicated to Louise-Mai Newberry, who knows it better than I do. Bu Ru! TBFC!

If You Don't Let Us Dream,
We Won't Let You Sleep

Characters
in order of appearance

McLean
Taylor
Thacker
Asset-Smith
Lucinda
Joan
Workman
Ryan
Man
Nurse
Administrator
McDonald
Jason
Ross
Teacher 1
Teacher 2
Thomas
Jen
Kelly
Zebedee
Ray

Shona translation by Lucian Msamati and Denton Chikura

Part One

Prologue

Darkness. The sounds of smashing glass and an alarm wailing. Running footsteps. Shouting. Laughter. A police siren in the distance. KRS-One's 'Sound of Da Police' starts up: 'Woop woop, that's the sound of da police/ Woop woop, that's the sound of the beast . . .'

Lights up on: a group of people in pinstriped suits and balaclavas robbing a bank, taking not just cash but paperwork, the office plants, the lot. Caught for a moment, they freeze, then get in formation and do a little dance to the music. The music stops. They rip off the balaclavas and assume a professional attitude round a table.

Scene One

Department of Home and Business Affairs. An expensively abstract logo on the wall.

McLean   Karen McLean, Department of Home and Business Affairs.

Taylor   Simon Taylor, Empathy Capital.

Thacker   Mick Thacker, Competitive Confinement Ltd.

Asset-Smith   James Asset-Smith. I believe you all know where I work.

Lucinda   Hi, I'm Lucinda, I make Delightful Chocolate. I mean, I don't make it, other people do, you know?

McLean   Good. Simon, it's your baby, why don't you christen it?

Taylor   Social dysfunction. Addiction. Depression. Violent crime. They cost this country tens of billions every year, expenses we simply can't afford in these austere times. The endless futile trek through courts, prisons, social workers, rehab and A&E. The pointless cycle of deprivation and dependency.

McLean   The *culture* of dependency. That's what we want to eradicate.

Thacker   Mmm. That 'I-want-something-for-nothing' disease.

Taylor   But what if there was a way to turn those burdens into opportunities? (*Holds up papers.*) Unity Bonds. Unity Bonds transfer the costs of social repair from the taxpayer to the private sector at a healthy return. Problem families can now be monetised, at a profit to investors and no cost to the public.

McLean   It's an incentive structure. The fewer people receive treatment for the problems, and/or the greater the reduction in offences, the higher the returns.

Taylor   It really is a game-changing solution.

They all subtly look at **Asset-Smith**. *He leafs through the papers. Beat.*

Asset-Smith   And investors bear the brunt of the costs?

McLean   With government underwriting. The usual arrangement.

Asset-Smith   What are the IRRs?

Taylor   Seven and a half per cent.

Asset-Smith   Seven and a half.

Taylor   To start with. At a minimum.

McLean   Capped at fifteen.

Asset-Smith   I've got Indian infrastructure and Chinese mines bringing in two or three times that.

McLean   Come on, James, we're talking about something *useful*.

Asset-Smith   And highly illiquid.

Thacker   I've got no problem with monetising social behaviour. It's the principle the private prison system is based on. My concern is if we were saddled with the impossible cases, the hard nuts. What does that do to our profit margins?

McLean   I think in order to get schemes like this off the ground, we can see our way clear to a certain number of exemptions.

Asset-Smith   I'd need no caps on profits, baselines on losses –

McLean   James –

Asset-Smith   You're up against private equity here. The pursuit of alpha returns. You either engage with that reality, or forget it. (*Beat.*) We'd also need bail-out guarantees and a controlling stake in how the bonds are administered.

McLean   That isn't the purview of the private sector –

Asset-Smith   Come on, Karen, you're not exactly bargaining from a position of strength, are you?

Pause.

McLean   I'm sure the model has space for development. Simon?

Taylor   Absolutely. It's all about commonality of interests.

Beat.

Asset-Smith   In which case I think it has considerable possibilities.

McLean   Excellent. Then let's proceed.

Lucinda   Sorry, I just . . . I know it's . . . What actually is a bond?

Taylor   What *is* it? What do you mean?

McLean   Lucinda is one of our Regenerator Innovators.

Taylor   Ohhh.

Lucinda (*gesturing at* **McLean**)   We're donating some money to –

Taylor   I've heard of the scheme, yes.

McLean   She's at 'Trailblazer' level, no less.

Lucinda   Once you've made a bit of money you want to do something with it, don't you? Something you can be proud of.

Taylor   I think that's how we all feel, yes.

McLean   A bond, Lucinda, pays off when a certain threshold is achieved. If the number of people who commit crimes or receive treatment for drug addiction goes down to a certain level, investors get a return. If not, they don't. It's all about harnessing the incentivising power of the market.

Beat. **Lucinda** *nods.*

Lucinda   I see. No, that sounds very . . . sensible.

They start to gather their papers.

Why doesn't the state pay for it?

McLean   Sorry?

Lucinda   From, you know, taxes.

They politely suppress their collective amusement. Beat.

Thacker   Delightful Chocolate? That's you, is it?

Lucinda   It is, yes.

Thacker   I've had the lemongrass and chilli. It's very nice.

Lucinda   Thank you.

They rise and go. As they leave, a quote is scribbled on the wall, then fades:

> Fascism should more properly be called corporatism, because it is the merger of state and corporate power.
> *Benito Mussolini*

Scene Two

An old woman, **Joan**, *sits. A* **Workman** *installs something behind her. Pause.*

Joan   I don't know how you can do it. (*Beat.*) I don't know how you can –

Workman   Nearly finished.

Joan   Like going back in time, it is. Be bringing back rationing next. Poorhouses.

Workman   Won't be long now.

Beat.

Joan   Fought a war for this. Fought a war for our rights.

Workman   You don't have a Phillips-head, do you?

Joan   Not the Germans. After that. A war against our lot. The elite.

Workman   Think I left mine in the van.

Joan   To be treated as human beings. To think of ourselves as human beings. We weren't used to it, y'see.

Workman (*holds up a screwdriver*)   Tell a lie. It was here all the time.

Joan   A place to call home. Food on the table. Why shouldn't we have them things? What's a society for unless to make sure people have them things? (*Beat.*) It's the way we treat each other now. Like threats. That's what I can't bear. We treat one another like threats. (*Beat.*) You probably aren't listening to a word I'm saying, are you?

Workman   Be out of your hair any minute now.

Joan   Have you got a granny? I said, have you got a – ?

Workman   I heard you.

Joan   Well?

Workman   It won't make it any easier on you, you know.

Joan   Answer the –

Workman   I have got a granny, yes.

Joan   And are you doing the same to her?

Workman   They're not, no.

Joan   Why not?

Workman   Because she pays the tax, as it happens.

Joan   Does she now?

Workman   She does, yes.

Joan   And how does she afford that?

Beat.

Workman   She lives with us.

Joan   Well, isn't she the lucky one?

Beat. He leans towards her.

Workman   Pay it.

Joan   Not mine to pay.

Workman   Everyone else is.

Joan   Didn't cause it, not paying for it.

Workman   It's only a one-off, they reckon.

Joan   For now.

Workman   Just pay it.

Joan   With what?

Beat. He fiddles for a short while then steps away. It's an electricity meter.

Workman   Right.

Joan   Done, is it?

Workman   It is, yeah.

Joan   Right-oh.

Workman   You put the money in here. It takes coins or notes. When you're about to run out, there's a beep and a red light starts to flash. (*Leafing through papers.*) Right then, Joan –

Joan   Mrs Thompson.

Workman   Your debt tax has been set at –

Joan   Five hundred and thirty-three pounds and sixty-three pence.

Workman   When that's paid –

Joan   Ninety-six pound fifty.

Workman   I'll be –

Joan   That's my pension. Ninety-six fifty a week. I was forty-two years a nurse. Looking after people.

She stares reproachfully at him. Beat.

Workman   When that's paid, I'll be right back to take the meter off again. Quick as you like. Call any time.

Joan   What if I don't pay?

Beat.

Workman   Please call. Number's on here, look.

Joan   Mind how you go.

He makes to leave, hesitates.

Workman   Eighteen months. Eighteen months tramping in the rain and standing in line, nothing. There's a way people look at you now when you're out of work, you'd think with more of us there'd be more solidarity, but it's the opposite. My nan with us. Three kids. My wife looking at me angle-eyed. Then this come up.

The meter beeps and a red light starts to flash.

You got any change?

Joan   You run along.

*The **Workman** digs in his pocket and pulls out some change.*

Workman   There's two quid, look. Get you started.

Joan   I don't want your money.

He puts the money down in front of her. Beat.

Workman   I'll be late for the next one.

He leaves. Pause. The red light flashes violently and the beep becomes a drawn-out screech.

Blackout. Silence.

Scene Three

Prison holding-cell. A young boy, **Ryan***, seated at a table. A large* **Man** *sits across from him holding a file. He wears a black leather jacket with the logo 'Competitive Confinement Ltd' across the back of it. The man flicks through the file. Pause.*

Ryan   It was nothing to do with me.

The **Man** *flicks through the file again. Beat.*

Ryan   It was nothing to do with me.

The **Man** *looks up and around the room.*

Man   There's an echo in here.

He eyeballs the boy. Pause.

Tell me what happened, Ryan.

Beat.

Ryan   There's this protest. Against these cunts trying to kick away the ladder –

Man   Leave the politics out of it, there's a good lad.

Ryan   And it gets a bit out of hand. People are fucking angry, you know what I mean, and there's one or two not there for the right reasons.

Man   Like Jason.

Ryan   He comes out JD's with a few boxes and hands 'em to me and says he'll be right back, he needs some size-fives for this yat he's got a ting with. I told him I didn't want nothing to do with it. There's a hand on my shoulder and I'm in here. No word of a lie, mate, that is what happened.

Pause.

Man   Bit of a prick. Jason.

Ryan   He's a mate of mine.

Man   He's done it before? Thieving?

The boy looks uncomfortable. Beat. The **Man** *flicks through the file.*

Man   Not a bad lad, are you? Not been inside before, no record with the police. Bright lad as well. Were you hoping to go to university?

Ryan   I am going to university.

Man   Are you, son? Good on you. Might be difficult now.

Ryan   I'm not that kind of person.

Man   No. You're not. The thing is, Ryan, that's why you're here.

Beat.

Ryan   What?

Man   Our job, what they pay us for now, is to reduce rates of reoffending. Your mate Jason, as you just admitted, is a serial offender. No chance of him stopping.

Ryan   Hang on a sec.

Man   Why should we be punished for that? For his moral turpitude?

Ryan   But he's the one –

Man   You, on the other hand, you're the decent type. You're not gonna do it again, are you?

Ryan   I didn't fucking do it this time!

Man   If you plead guilty –

Ryan   They weren't my –

Man   If you plead guilty, bearing in mind the relatively minor nature of the crime, I'd see you getting a very short custodial sentence. Three months maybe.

Ryan   Fuck off! Three months –

Man   In return for which we'd write you the most glowing reference you can imagine. After all, we have what our website calls a 'commonality of interests'. If you come back here after you get out, we don't get paid.

Beat as the boy gathers himself.

Ryan   One more time, mate, yeah: they weren't mine.

Man   Or you can put that claim to a judge. It's quite a hostile environment out there at the minute. They were in your hands when you were arrested, Ryan. (*Beat.*) You don't have to decide now. I'll see you again in the morning.

He gets up and starts to leave. He stops and puts his hand on the boy's shoulder.

One more thing. If you do take up our offer and I see you back in here, I will come to your cell one night when you are sleeping, and I will pour battery acid over your face. OK? (*Beat.*) There'll be someone along to take you upstairs in a few minutes.

He leaves. The boy stares into space. Blackout.

Scene Four

Joan *in A&E. Strip lighting, plastic seats, dirty linoleum floor. A hubbub of languages and screaming kids grates on her ears. She holds her arm close. Blood seeps through a dressing. A harassed **Nurse** enters and attends to someone else.*

Joan   Nurse. (*Beat.*) Nurse. (*Beat.*) Nurse.

Nurse (*not looking*)   Sorry, I'm dealing with another patient.

Beat.

Joan   Nurse. Excuse me, nurse?

Nurse   What is it?

Joan   How much longer?

Nurse   We're very busy at present.

Joan   Half an hour? An hour?

Nurse   I couldn't say. A couple of hours maybe.

Joan   It hurts.

The **Nurse** *gets up and leaves. She returns a short while later with an aspirin, a plastic cup of water and a sheaf of papers.*

Nurse   There you go.

Joan   Thank you. (*She takes the aspirin with the water.*) What are these?

Nurse   Forms you need to fill in.

Joan   I filled in a load before.

Nurse   Different lot. That was Unity, this is the care trust.

Joan   Why do they need different lots?

Nurse   Efficiency.

She goes to another patient. The old woman writes but it causes too much pain.

Joan   It's this bloody bandage is the problem. It's not on right, I can tell. Can you have another look at it, nurse? It's . . .

The **Nurse** *comes and fiddles with the bandage. The old woman moans.*

Nurse   How'd you do it?

Joan   Trying to fix something. Smash something, more like.

Nurse   Should know better at your age.

Joan   Smash that bloody box off my electricity them thieving parasites put on.

*The **Nurse**'s manner changes abruptly. She drops **Joan**'s arm.*

Nurse   That's the best I can do for you, I'm afraid.

Joan   What d'you mean, that's the best you can do?

Nurse   It's not my area.

Joan   Not your area? What kind of a nurse are you, can't do a simple bandage?

Nurse   I'm not a nurse, as it happens.

Joan   Not a . . . ?

Nurse   I'm a volunteer. I don't have to be here. I'm trying to do my bit.

Joan   What are you then, if you're not a nurse?

Beat.

Nurse   I work for an electricity company.

An administrator enters, holding papers.

Administrator   Joan, is it?

Joan   Mrs Thompson.

Administrator   I'm afraid we can't make provision for you at this hospital, Joan.

Joan   Why not?

Administrator   It's an insufficiently serious injury to justify –

Joan   It's a laceration with subcutaneous hematoma –

Administrator   What I mean is, given our exceptionally high –

Joan   I've always come to this hospital.

Administrator   – *exceptionally* high patient volume, you'd be better off looking –

Joan   I used to *work* in this hospital.

Administrator   We can't make provision for you.

Joan   Why not?

Beat.

Administrator   Unity rejected your application.

Joan   I didn't make an application. I didn't *make* an 'application'.

Administrator   I'm very sorry, Joan. Please accept my sincere –

Joan   Why'd they turn me down?

Administrator   I couldn't say, it's a matter of commercial –

Joan   Tell me that. Tell me that and I'll get out of your hair.

Beat.

Administrator   Unity incentives are based on the reduction of waiting lists. One rather effective way to achieve that is not to let people on them.

Joan   I see.

Administrator   I really am sorry, but I am going to have to ask you to leave.

He leaves. She stews. An African man, **McDonald Moyo**, *enters leaning on the nurse, bleeding heavily. She sits him next to* **Joan**. *The* **Administrator** *enters.*

Administrator   Papers? Do you have insurance papers? Doesn't seem to speak much English. Insurance? (*French.*) Assurance?

Nurse   *Seguro?*

Administrator   *Assicurazione?*

Nurse   *Bima?*

Administrator   *Страхование?* (*Strakovanye?*) ‫أت‬‫؟‬‫نيمأت‬ (*Tamin?*)

McDonald *pulls some papers from his pocket and hands them to the* **Administrator**, *who looks them over briefly and nods.*

Administrator   He's next.

He leaves. **McDonald** *leans back, clutching his side. Pause.*

Joan (*to* **McDonald**)   Bet you think you're clever. Bet you think you're right clever. Coming in waving them around. (*Beat.*) What gives you the right to jump over me? What gives you the right to bloody be here at all?

He says something placatory.

Don't you talk back to me! Don't you talk to me, you sod! Parasite! Why don't you piss off back where you come from, get them to look after you? Go on, piss off. (*She stands. Beat.*) I hope you bloody die.

Blackout.

Scene Five

A Wetherspoon's in a satellite town. **Ryan** *and two of his mates,* **Jason** *and* **Ross***, quite drunk, screaming at a screen with WKD alcopops in front of them.*

Jason   You *cunt*! You useless fucking cunt!

Ross   Two yards out!

Ryan   Fucking spastic!

A whistle on screen. Groans of disappointment from the punters around.

Jason   FUCK!

Ryan   That's two points thrown away.

Ross   I told you he was shit when we signed him.

Jason   FUCKING BLACK CUNT.

He lunges for a WKD and knocks it to the floor. Somebody shouts 'Wahey!'

Ross   Call Autoglass, somebody's smashed.

Jason   Your round.

Ross   What? I just –

Jason   Your round.

Beat. **Ross** *gets up and goes.* **McDonald** *pushes on a mop and bucket and starts to clean up the mess.* **Jason** *watches him. Beat.*

Jason   Here's another one, look.

Ryan   For fuck's sake, Jase.

Jason   Oy, mate? Mate?

McDonald *looks up at him.*

Jason   Be a top African and get some water for the boys? Wa–ter. Yeah, be a top African and fetch us some.

Beat. **McDonald** *takes a step towards the bar.*

Jason   Not from there. Do like you usually do. (*Kicks bucket.*) Put that on your head and take it to the watering hole.

Ryan   Jase.

Jason   What? I'm only having a bit of banter with him. I'll have mine without any AIDS in it, please mate. And no hippo shit. Yeah? Nice one.

Ross *returns with three more WKDs.* **McDonald** *cautiously returns to the mess.*

Ross   What's he on about?

Ryan   Gone off on one again.

Jason   Mate, mate, listen to this: I adopted an African child, yeah? I was worried he wouldn't adapt to our way of life, so I installed a treadmill in front of the sink.

Ross   Got that one off Sickipedia.

Jason   Laugh then, ya black cunt.

McDonald *gets up and leaves.*

Ryan   Fuck's sakes, John Terry.

Jason   What? I wouldn't complain if someone called me a white cunt.

Ross   Cos it's true.

Jason   So what's he complaining about?

Ryan   Cos maybe it's –

Jason   I knew you was gonna say that. It's not fucking 'racist', it's a *description*. Like Ross just got a round of drinks in, Africans go get a bucket of water in.

Ross   Fair play.

Jason   How d'you kill a hundred flies? Smash an African in the face with a shovel.

Ross   Alright, Farmer Giles.

Jason   Eh?

Ross *(making 'milking cow' gestures)*   Fucking milking it now.

Ryan   Fucking Gold Top.

Ross   Get a float, mate.

Jason   What are you laughing at? It's cunts like him that's why you're here.

Ross   Mate, I'm here to get battered and watch the footie.

Jason   You know what I mean. (*To* **Ryan**.) He's got your job.

Ryan   I don't wanna wash floors.

Jason   You wanna fucking do something. Thumb up your arse all day like –

Ryan   I'm going to universi –

Jason (*slamming down his WKD hard on the table*)   *Don't* fucking –

Ryan   I am –

Jason   Stop with that shit. Stop it.

Ross   Ah, let him –

Jason   You're deluding yourself. You are, Ryan. Nobody fucking wants you.

Ross   'Ckin hell, Jase, that's harsh.

Jason   They don't though. Who wants him? Nothing kid, been inside, *English*, who gives a fuck about him? What they want, son, is cunts like him.

Ryan   He's washing floors, mate.

Ross   He is right though, Ryan.

Jason   Go up London. Africans in big headdresses swanning out of Harrods. Chinks in fucking suits and ties, stuffing their faces in the posh restaurants. Arab cunts with their postbox birds mincing up and down King's Road with ten shopping bags in each hand. Go up London, that's all you see. Everyone, *everyone's* got a piece of the pie except for us and I am sick and fucking tired of it. I am sick and fucking tired of –

Ryan   I am going to uni –

Jason (*in his face*)   You fucking get a grip. You *fucking* get a grip. (*Beat.*) It is us against them. Nobody in this world gives a flying fuck about you apart from the people round this table. That's the truth, Ryan. The sooner you get your thick head around that, the better off you'll be.

McDonald *appears with the bucket on his head.*

Jason   Oy oy!

Ross   Oy oy!

He walks towards them with an exaggerated servility, limping and cringing.

Ryan   Oh my days!

Ross   Yes, my son!

Jason   That is a top African. That is one who knows his place.

Ross   Get in!

Jason   That is a nigger who knows his –

McDonald *throws the bucket of water over* **Jason***. A beat of calm before the storm.*

Ryan   Oh shit.

Blackout.

Scene Six

A nursery. Brightly coloured scribbles on the walls. A teacher stands with a piece of paper. Pause. Another teacher enters. Beat.

Teacher 1   How is she?

Teacher 2   She's fine. Playing.

Teacher 1   Does she . . . ?

Teacher 2   I don't think so, no.

Teacher 1   What's she saying?

Teacher 2   Not saying anything. Just playing. Peppa Pig.

Teacher 1   Did you get through?

Teacher 2   The phone's still off. Been off for the past hour.

Teacher 1   Shit.

Teacher 2   Did you speak to Social Services?

Beat.

Teacher 1   I mean, there's quite a few you can tell are struggling. Kim's mum.

Teacher 2   Mmm. Hair.

Teacher 1   Danielle's. Crying in the street the other day about the state of Danielle's coat. But not her. Never late. Make-up always nice.

Teacher 2   Bit tarty for me, to be fair.

Teacher 1   Always polite.

Teacher 2   Fancies herself a bit.

Teacher 1   Always time for a chat.

Teacher 2   How d'you reckon she chose?

Beat.

Teacher 1   Chose?

Teacher 2   She's got three, doesn't she? So how d'you reckon she chose? (*Beat.*) Read it again. Doesn't say about the other two. Just says about Anna.

Teacher 1 *reads the note again.*

Teacher 1   Call her again.

Teacher 2   Her phone's off.

Teacher 1   And go check up on Anna. Please.

Beat. **Teacher 2** *leaves.* **Teacher 1** *reads the note again. Pause.* **Teacher 2** *re-enters. She shakes her head.*

Teacher 2   How do you tell a three-year-old girl she's the one her mother left behind?

Beat.

Teacher 1   Where's the dad?

Teacher 2   Gone with her, I expect. Lost his job, didn't he? He was fitting those debt tax meters.

Teacher 1   Alright, this is what we're going to do. You stay with her. I'll pop out to the shops –

Teacher 2   The thing is, Jess –

Teacher 1   Get her a change of / clothes

Teacher 2   I've got a date.

Beat.

Teacher 1   *What?*

Teacher 2   With that guy. Jason. I told you about it.

Teacher 1 (*pointing at the room*)   There's a – !

Teacher 2   Call Social Services –

Teacher 1   And you're talking / about

Teacher 2   They'll –

Teacher 1   I called them. I called them, OK?

Teacher 2   And? What'd they say?

Teacher 1   They won't take her.

Teacher 2   They've got to, don't they?

Teacher 1   Apparently not.

Teacher 2   Why not?

Teacher 1   She'd put them over their incentives.

Pause.

Teacher 2   I've got to go.

Teacher 1   You're not / serious?

Teacher 2   I've done my job, my job finished an hour ago, and this is not my fault –

Teacher 1   She's three years old, Rachel.

Teacher 2   It's not my fault, OK? I do my job bloody well for hardly nothing and I never meet anyone and he's really nice. I got a dress special. (*Beat.*) I'm sorry, love. He's really nice. You'll like him.

Scene Seven

Asset-Smith *behind his desk in his spacious office. A trader,*
Thomas, *in front of him. Over them plays Cameron's speech after the*
2011 riots:

Cameron *(recorded)*   'There is a complete lack of responsibility
in parts of our society. People allowed to feel that the world
owes them something, that their rights outweigh their
responsibilities and their actions do not have consequences.
Well, they do have consequences.'

Pause.

Asset-Smith   We short rape.

Beat.

Thomas   What?

Asset-Smith   Senior rape, mezzanine rape, junior. We short
all of it.

Thomas   But –

Asset-Smith   Crime, depression, illiteracy. All the Unity
stuff. Set up new markets in all of them. OTC derivatives
should do it. I've already reached out to a few pension funds,
institutional investors. Lots of interest. *(Beat.)* Problem?

Thomas   What's the pitch?

Asset-Smith   Say it's a hedge. We're long the initial
investment, we're hedging.

Thomas   What kind of volume?

Asset-Smith   Start with a couple of bill and go up from
there.

Thomas *(whistles)*   That's not a hedge, that's a twelve-foot
ornamental shrubbery carved into the shape of a giant
fucking peacock.

Asset-Smith   Alright?

Thomas   Yeah, fine.

Beat.

Asset-Smith   You don't understand.

Thomas   Course I do.

Asset-Smith   But you don't want to admit it.

Beat.

Thomas   We put all that time and money into setting them up, I just –

Asset-Smith   A rape bond, or a crime bond, or an addiction bond, Thomas, pays out when the number of rapes or crimes or addictions is reduced, am I correct?

Thomas   I don't need a lesson in –

Asset-Smith   Sorry, did you make partner recently? Congratulations. Someone should have told me. (*Beat.*) In other words, Unity bonds are a bet on social harmony. Look out of this window. Do you see a rise in social harmony on the horizon? Is that angry roaring noise in fact the sound of an enormous number of colourful butterflies?

Thomas   I get the point, James.

Asset-Smith   Social discord seems the safer bet. An almost guaranteed bet, in fact. It would be a dereliction of my duty to shareholders not to make that bet. Short fucking rape.

Thomas   What about the . . . ?

He trails off. Beat.

Asset-Smith   What about the what?

Thomas   Nothing. (*Beat.*) The social utility factor. You're basically asking for a rise in –

Asset-Smith   I'm not asking for a rise in anything. I'm responding to simple reality. If we could make sufficient returns on a reduction in crime, I would do it. That is why I invested in the initial scheme. It would appear we can make

better returns on an increase in crime. It's not the job of
markets to shape the world. (*Beat.*) It's nothing personal,
Thomas. I hope you understand that.

Thomas   We invented Unity. Do we not have a
responsibility to – ?

Asset-Smith   Markets are not responsible to anyone. That
is their peculiar beauty. It's what makes them free. (*Beat. Looks
at his BlackBerry.*) I'll see you in the pub later, Thomas.

Blackout.

Scene Eight

Ryan *in a prison cell. Pause. His door opens and the* **Man** *in the
black leather jacket fills it. In his hand is a bottle that looks like it
contains chemicals. Pause.*

Man   Evening. (*He holds up the bottle.*) Thirsty?

Ryan   Get out of my cell.

The **Man** *sniffs the bottle and recoils.*

Man   Wouldn't wanna drink that. Use it to clean your toilet,
maybe.

He jerks the bottle at **Ryan**, *who flinches.*

Man   I told you I'd see you again. Didn't I?

Ryan   Don't.

Man   Here I am. And I brought you something.

Ryan   Don't!

The **Man** *throws some of the contents of the bottle over* **Ryan**, *who
screams in fear. Beat. The* **Man** *sips from the bottle and holds it out to
the boy.*

Man   Mineral water. The water in here is very hard. (*Beat.*)
You're a lucky boy, Ryan. You fucked up. I asked you to do

one simple thing and you fucked it up. Luckily for you, priorities have changed.

Ryan   You lied to me.

Man   Not too bad in here, is it? You'll get used to it soon.

Ryan   You lied to me!

Man   The thing you've got to understand, Ryan, is the public won't wear it. Very little appetite out there right now for hard-luck stories. A lot of people are having a tough time, but *they're* not stabbing hardworking immigrants in unprovoked attacks, being a burden on the state, costing taxpayers' money. You should see the polls. Very much against you. Very much against you, Ryan.

Beat.

Ryan   What do you *want*?

Man   I want you not to have any hope. (*Beat.*) I want you not to lose yourself in any delusions. It's important that one sees oneself for what one truly is. One of the hardest things to achieve in life. To cut through the fog of delusions and aspirations and dreams, to really plant your feet on the hard rock of reality. Hardly any of us manage it. We're away with the fairies, living in the future, a world of things to come that probably never will. In that sense, Ryan, you're quite lucky. Here, within the rough concrete embrace of these four walls, you truly know who and what you are.

Beat. He moves back to the door.

Good talking to you.

Ryan   You lied to me.

Man   I'll be downstairs if you ever want to chat again.

Ryan   You told me if I went guilty you'd –

Man   The thing is, Ryan: priorities have changed.

Blackout.

Scene Nine

Department for Home and Business Affairs. **McLean**, *better dressed.*
Lucinda *enters.*

Lucinda   Karen, hi!

McLean   Lucinda, good to see you. Thanks for coming in.
The others should be here any minute.

Lucinda   You look different.

McLean   Really?

Lucinda   Mmm.

McLean   It's the diet, I expect. Managed to stick to it for a
change.

Lucinda   How much have you lost?

McLean   Only half a stone, but it's how you carry it, isn't it?

Beat.

Lucinda   This should be fun.

McLean   Fun?

Lucinda   Exciting. To hear people's opinions.

McLean   Oh, I think I know what they're going to say. I
mean it's been an enormous success.

Lucinda   Has it?

McLean   Hasn't it?

Lucinda   Oh no, I didn't mean to suggest –

McLean   We've exceeded all initial expectations. The
returns have been quite spectacular. And there's an absolute
deluge of interest in the new offerings.

Lucinda   The new . . . ?

McLean   The second phase. (*Beat.*) It was always the intent
to extend Unity into more abstract realms. Biodiversity.

Reproduction. Areas that are inherently more difficult to monetarise.

Lucinda   I'm not sure I –

McLean   It's more difficult to put a price on clean air or children, to establish a monetary value for happiness or truth. But not impossible. With the right model.

Lucinda   But they've failed, haven't they?

McLean   I'm sorry?

Lucinda   The bonds have failed.

Beat.

McLean   You have a rather odd definition of failure, Lucinda.

Lucinda   They didn't actually bring down crime. Or depression. Or rape.

McLean   Saving the state, and therefore the taxpayer, billions in payouts.

Lucinda   Those things have gone *up*.

McLean   And generated, via the derivatives market, a cascade of new revenues to deal with those issues. Simon, for example, is planning to make four or five new investments off the returns generated by the last one. The sky's the limit.

Beat.

Lucinda   I think I'm being thick.

McLean   I mean, these *are* complex financial models.

Lucinda   No, it's . . . But then it goes round and round for ever and you –

McLean   – turn social problems into an endless motor for growth. Correct. You spin the grubby cotton of common lives into golden thread. You give ordinary people, most of whom, let's face it, have no future as consumers in this society, let alone as workers, you give those people a purpose.

Lucinda   To get arrested. To drink. To fail.

McLean   You give people back their productive role. And thus their *dignity*.

Lucinda   You're making human weakness into raw material for financial speculation.

McLean   Well, what else can you do with it? At least it's not costing us money. (*Beat.*) It's when you give the market its head that you really start to see a difference, Lucinda. That you have, in your words, something to be proud of.

Pause.

Lucinda   You have to do something.

McLean   No.

Lucinda   Review it. Stop it.

McLean   I'm not in any position –

Lucinda   Of course you are, you're the government, none of this –

McLean   You misunderstand me, I –

Lucinda   This financial wizardry –

McLean   I'm –

Lucinda   – can work without public money.

McLean   I'm no longer in government, Lucinda. An opportunity arose in the private sector that I felt was . . . Where I felt I could do more good.

Lucinda   What are you – ?

McLean   I've replaced James. He's moved on to bigger things.

Beat.

Lucinda   I want my money back.

McLean   That's entirely your prerogative. I will just say that times like these, difficult times, are when we can least afford grandstanding.

Taylor *and* **Thacker** *enter.*

McLean   Good. Come in. Coffee on the left, tea on the right. Before we start, I believe Lucinda has something she wants to share with you. Over to you, Lucinda.

Pause.

Lucinda   I brought everyone some chocolate.

She holds out some bars of chocolate.

Blackout.

Scene Ten

Joan's *flat. In darkness, lit by a few guttering candles. Obviously cold –* **Joan** *and her companion,* **McDonald***, are wrapped heavily in tatty blankets. They hold mugs of tea. Over the top, Cameron again, his speech of January 2012:*

Cameron (*recorded*)   'I believe that open markets and free enterprise are the best imaginable force for improving human wealth and happiness. They are the engine of progress, generating the enterprise and innovation that lifts people out of poverty and gives people opportunity. And I would go further: where they work properly, open markets and free enterprise can actually promote morality.'

Pause.

Joan   Comfy?

Beat.

Another blanket?

Beat.

I'm sorry about the cold. There's wood for cooking and there's wood for heating but not always enough for both.

Beat.

Could be worse. Could be downstairs. In the basement. I was born in a basement.

Beat.

You have to be grateful, I suppose. Small mercies.

Beat.

You're very easy to talk to. A good listener. I'm glad of that.

Beat.

Took me a long time to find you. That terrible place. Wetherspoon's.

Beat.

I just wanted to say: I'm not that kind of person. That's all I wanted to say, really. They made me so angry in that hospital they made me not myself. It burned me acid inside like a digested penny after. What I said to you.

Beat.

Thank you, then. For letting me apologise.

Beat. **McDonald** *stirs.*

McDonald   *Zvinoshamisa! Haisi nguva refu yapfuura pandanga ndive ne mukadzi wangu ne vana vangu - ndiinawo mumaoko angu – ndiinawo ndichi va fema. Iye zvino, handi chambo gona kuvafunga. Rangariro yavo yangove se chiutsi, se bhayiscop ye upenyu we mumwe munhu. Handichaziva zvakaita vana vangu, handichaziva hwema hwe mukadzi wangu. Murume anokanganwa hwema we mukadzi wake sei? Vana vaakarera mumaoko ake. Pane zvinhu zvino nyanyo nyadzisa mu nyika muno, ku kokotama ne kupemha serombe zvinhu zvinofanira zviri zvangu se nhaka! Ku kanganwa chinhu chakabva mumapako angu, chiri muviri wangu, ndizvo zvino ndi sisimutsa.*

[It's very strange. Only a short while ago I was with my wife and children, I held them and breathed them. And now I can only remember them through a haze, as if they were images on screen from someone else's life. I cannot remember what my children feel like, what my wife smells like. How can a man forget his wife's smell? What he has held in his hands? Of all the humiliations here, the stooping and the begging for things that should be mine by rights, to forget the feeling of something that came of my body, that is my body, is the worst.]

Joan   You're talking about your wife and kids.

McDonald   You speak Shona?

Joan   It's obvious. The way you move your hands.

Beat.

McDonald   I am a structural engineer. BSc (Hons) from the University of Zimbabwe.

Joan   That's very impressive.

McDonald   BSc (Hons)!

Pause. His anger subsides into sadness.

This is the first time any English person has invited me into their home.

Beat.

Joan   I'll make you a new cup of tea.

Beat.

McDonald   Thank you.

Blackout.

Part Two

A beautiful wood-panelled courtroom – judge's bench, witness stand, jury – in a state of serious disrepair. A light hangs by wires, floorboards are loose and there's junk all over the place. A solid oak door, locked, guards the entrance. Above the bench hangs a banner in massive black letters:

THE COURT OF PUBLIC OPINION

Jen, *a veteran activist in her forties, sits with a mug of rooibos tea, bleeding from a head wound.* **Kelly**, *early thirties, new to the movement, cleans and bandages it.*

Kelly   Keep still.

Jen   Aah.

Kelly   Sorry.

Jen   'Salright.

Kelly   Nearly finished.

Beat.

Jen   I was on trial here.

Kelly   Serious?

Jen   Twyford Down, I think it was. '91?

Kelly   I was nine.

Jen   Or Reclaim the Streets. We were the last batch before they shut it down.

Kelly   How long did you get?

Jen   Three months. 'Assault on a policewoman'.

Kelly   Did you do it?

Jen   I did, yeah.

Kelly   Why?

Jen   Because she'd been stamping on my face. Two big buggers held me down in a chokehold and she stamped. For a good few minutes. Broke my nose in four places. When they let me go, I got up, wiped the blood off my face, and smacked her in the teeth.

Kelly   Wow. OK.

Jen   It was all worth it for the surprise in her eyes.

Kelly   I've never hit a girl.

Jen   She wasn't a girl.

Kelly   What did the judge say?

Jen   He didn't believe me. Nobody ever believes what the police do until (a) they've been battered on a demo, or (b) they've seen footage of someone else being battered on a demo.

Kelly   That's what got me into it. Watching the Tomlinson killing on YouTube.

Jen   The best protection against pro-corporate police violence isn't Amnesty International, it's a mobile phone with a camera in it. Made by a corporation. The world, Kelly, is a complex place. Ow.

Kelly   There you go.

Jen *springs to her feet.*

Kelly   How do you keep going?

Jen   How'd you mean?

Kelly   Twenty years of this.

Jen   And the rest.

Kelly   How do you do it?

Jen   Easy. You keep plugging away and you never give up and you keep fighting. I'm not special, Kel. Anyone can do it.

I'm just lucky I enjoy it, I suppose. (*Twigs.*) The Criminal Justice Bill, that was it. 'A succession of repetitive beats'.

Kelly   Eh?

Jen   Bloody hell, you are young, arentcha?

Kelly (*grinning*)   No, you're old.

Jen   The Criminal Justice Bill wanted to ban all music characterised by a succession of repetitive beats.

Kelly (*indicates* **Jen***'s head*)   Ironically, what the police just did to you.

Jen   I'm thinking of opening a Met Police-themed health spa.

Kelly   Isn't all music characterised by a succession of repetitive beats?

Jen   The 'Ian Tomlinson' head-and-body massage. The 'Jean Charles de Menezes' special acupuncture.

Kelly   Slogan: 'You'll think you died and went to heaven.'

Jen   That's good, I'll have that. (*They smile at each other.*) Right, enough wittering: where are we?

Kelly   Al-Jazeera's coming.

Jen   I would expect no less.

Kelly   Someone from *Guardian* 'Comment is Free'.

Jen   I *hate Guardian* 'Comment is Free'. Particularly the comments. They drain me of the will to live.

Kelly   And the *Mail* is coming, 'to see if we're the dirty layabouts everyone says we are'. I *think* she meant it ironically.

Jen   Al-Jazeera, the *Guardian* and the *Mail*: together at last.

Kelly   There's a good few others showing interest. You lot getting battered can't hurt. Metaphorically speaking. Loads of retweets, blog hits . . . It's building up.

Jen   How many people coming, do you reckon?

Kelly (*shrugs*)   Couple of hundred, maybe.

Jen   Then we'd better crack on.

She stares at her fingers. There is blood on them. Beat.

Kelly   Are you OK, Jen?

Jen's *façade slips a little and distress peeks through. She stifles it. Beat.*

Jen   My own fault. You'd think I'd know better after all these years. Never turn your back on the cunts.

Enter **Zebedee**, *a 'professional' activist wearing an Anonymous mask (the Guy Fawkes one from* V for Vendetta.*) and* **Joan**, *the old woman from the first part.*

Zebedee (*muffled by the mask*)   Toilets are done.

Jen   Take off the mask.

Zebedee (*muffled*)   The point of the mask –

Jen   I'm aware of the point of the mask, Zeb. It's to maintain anonymity and enhance the power of the collective. No one else is wearing one right now, which isn't doing wonders for your anonymity. I've got a headache. Take off the mask.

Zebedee *takes his mask off.*

Zebedee   Fucking disgrace.

Joan   I still think you should report it.

Jen   Who to? If you're gonna say 'the police', there's a tiny flaw in your plan.

Joan   The press? I don't see why they should get away –

Jen   Can we stop talking about it? Please? Hazards of the trade. If you can't take it, don't be here. Where are we?

Zebedee   Toilets are done.

Joan (*wrinkling her nose*)   Done as they'll ever be.

Zebedee   Fair point.

Jen   Lights?

Zebedee   No.

Jen   Floorboards?

Zebedee *kicks a loose floorboard.*

Jen   Come on! We've got no time!

Joan   We're waiting for Ray to bring the tools.

Jen   Well where is he?

A knock on the big wooden doors.

Ray (*off*)   It's me.

Kelly (*with some affection*)   Speak of the devil.

Zebedee (*calls out*)   'It's been a long time, I shouldn't have left you.'

Ray (*off*)   It's me.

Zebedee   'It's been a long time, I shouldn't have – '

Ray (*off*)   Open the fucking door.

Jen   Let him in.

Zebedee *opens the door to let in* **Ray**, *an Irishman in his twenties, followed by* **Ryan**, *the young boy from Part One, and an unexpected arrival:* **Thomas**, *the former trader, dressed down. He looks about in amazement.*

Zebedee (*to* **Ray**)   The correct response is, 'Without a strong rhyme to step to'.

Ray   Who made that shite the password anyway? (*To* **Ryan**.) 'Ne'er-do-well'. That was the horse.

Ryan   Fair play.

Jen   Let's get to work.

Ray *starts chucking hammers, screwdrivers, etc. to people while recounting his tale to the room. People grab the tools and start fixing the walls and flooring.*

Ray   Who wouldn't back a horse called Ne'er-do-well? It's a plain double bluff. Twenty to one, dead fucking cert.

Ryan (*grinning*)   Standard.

Ray   I plonk down twenty pound, the fucking thing goes down like a sniper's hit it five yards from the line. I says to the bookie, I'm willing to take a fifty per cent haircut on that bet. 'Excuse me?' says your man. I says, I'm a core investor in your firm, let's diversify risk, give me ten quid back and we'll say no more about it. The eedjit calls over security! You clearly don't understand how the global economy functions these days, my son.

He spots **Jen***'s face for the first time.*

Ray   Jesus, what happened to you?

Jen   They cleaned us out of the square.

Ray   Are you fucking serious?

Jen   Get to work, Ray.

Ray   But –

Kelly *pulls at his arm and he goes quiet for a moment. The rest work for a few beats.* **Thomas** *wanders, hammer in hand.* **Ryan** *and* **Joan** *working together.*

Ryan   You seem to know what you're doing, Joanie.

Joan   I've always loved work. It's the thing that makes me feel most real.

Ryan   You're good at it.

Joan   My father was a carpenter.

Ray   Tommy, over here, son.

Tom   Sorry, mate. It's mad here. I've not seen anything like it.

Ray   Everyone, I've news.

Joan   You seem to have the knack yourself.

Ryan   Done a coupla courses.

Ray   There's good news and bad news. Or good news, good news and bad news. Or is it good news, bad news and good news?

Joan   College courses?

Ryan (*uncomfortable*)   College, yeah.

Ray   The good news is we've been declared terrorists.

Jen   What?

Ray (*unfolds a piece of paper*)   Leak from the plod: terrorism update for the City of London Business 'Community'. High-level terror threats to the City of London: the Revolutionary Armed Forces of Colombia, who last I heard were mainly known for their exploits in *Colombia*, thus the name; Al Qaeda; and us.

Jen   Fuckers. *Fuckers.*

Kelly   How is this the good news?

Ray   Shows we're doing our job, getting under their skin. They can't get rid of us so they have to call us names.

Ryan   Trust.

Ray   Solve some real crimes, ya fat plod fucknuts! The true crimes of the modern world, the ones that rob millions of people not just one or two, take place in the big shiny glass towers down the road. LIBOR-rigging. Gas-market rigging. Google and Vodaphone dodging billions in taxes. Mubarak depended on the City of London. So did AIG and Lehman Brothers. Every non-dom dictator and Russian klepto-plutocrat rinses their filthy money clean through the London Stock Exchange – the Jordanian army is listed on the London Stock Exchange, for fuck's sake! – but oh no, *we're* the terrorists, get the armed response unit down the protest camp pronto in case someone gets stabbed with a sharpened lentil.

Kelly   So what's the bad news?

Ray   The bad news is I've decided not to be the defence.

General hubbub.

Jen   *What?*

Zebedee   We voted you the defence, Ray.

Ray   The good news part of the bad news is I've found the perfect replacement.

He pushes **Thomas** *gently forward.*

Tom   What?

Kelly   What?!

Ray (*innocent*)   What? You said you wanted to help.

Tom   No, I'm not –

Zebedee   You can't just decide –

Ray   Ah, it's grand –

Jen   It is not 'grand' –

Ray   Tell 'em where you're from, Tommy.

Tom   I'm just here –

Kelly   You can't do this, Ray.

Zebedee   We *voted* you –

Ray   Tommy used to work for Goldman Sachs.

Zebedee   Oh, fucking brilliant.

Ray   He's the perfect fella to defend them.

Tom   Defend who from what?

Zebedee   A spy? You've brought in a fucking spy?

Tom   I'm not a spy. What kind of spy says who he's spying for?

Zebedee   A fucking . . . clever spy? A double-bluff spy?

Tom   Look, I just came down here to see what all the fuss was about.

Jen (*to* **Ray**)   You will do your job.

Ray (*gesturing at* **Tom**)   Your man here is ten times better qualified –

Jen   You will do your fucking job, Ray. For once in your life you will do something that isn't whatever you want to do.

Ray   Don't fuckin' tell me –

Jen   You swan about like it's all a bit of a laugh –

Ray   You don't even know me, Jen.

Jen   Terrorism is not a laugh. It's how they fucked us before. Ten, twelve years ago, we had them running. I honestly thought the world was never going to be the same. J18, Seattle, Genoa: the anti-globalisation protests, hundreds of thousands of people looking for something new, beyond the old dead lies of nation and state and market. A radically new world. And then came 9/11.

Ray   Jen, I respect what you've done in the past, but –

Jen   And it all died. People got scared, and every fucker was suddenly an expert on the evils of Islam, and all the old dead ideas grabbed us by the throat again. It's taken ten years to get the poisonous lie of terrorism out of our bloodstream. So what's the first thing they try to do? I will not let them shut us up this time. And that means, Ray, that we take this seriously.

Beat.

Ray   Have you been to Ireland?

Jen   No, but I –

Ray   Sitting here drinking your rooibos fucking tea –

Kelly Ray –

Jen I'm not trying to –

Ray D'you know what the worst of Ireland is, Jen? It's not the joblessness. Nor the rake of never-to-be-finished houses looming over you like scaffolds. It's the guilt. The giving in and the guilt. Ireland was bankrupted by fifteen men. There's fifteen property speculators owe Anglo Irish half a billion apiece and all the rest of us'll be choking on that for life and nobody says a thing because, for some literally insane reason, *we* feel guilty. Like somehow it's *our* fault we got robbed, because we had the temerity to want a little happiness. We had something beyond the cold creak of the church door, just for a moment, and then the greatest theft since Cromwell, and now every family of four is carrying two hundred thousand euros of someone else's debt and how in God's name are they supposed to pay it? There's a loss of life, a whole world of what could have been that's being strangled and *nobody will fight back*, and I'm as committed to this thing as anyone but if you think I'm going to say a single word in defence of those murderers you'd better think again, long and hard.

Pause.

Zebedee Coffee, anyone?

Ryan I'll come with ya.

Tom I'm gonna head off I think.

Kelly Ryan, can you go?

Ryan Alright.

He slips away.

Kelly Tommy . . . is it Tommy?

Tom Tom.

Kelly Please stay. Just for a few minutes. We could really use you.

The rest gather into a circle. **Tom** *hesitates a moment, then decides to see what's going to happen.* **Ray** *refuses.*

Ray   A meeting? Another fucking meeting?

Kelly   Shut up and sit down.

Ray   I did not join a revolutionary autonomist organisation to sit in fucking meetings.

Kelly   You are making a twat out of yourself.

Jen   Right, so the first question is: do we still want to do the trial?

Zebedee *and* **Joan** *make the signal for agreement: fingers up, palms out, hands waved from side to side.*

Tom   What's with the jazz hands?

Joan   It's how you say yes without saying 'yes'.

Tom   It makes you look like a Marcel Marceau tribute group.

Joan   It gives everyone a chance to speak. Not just the men with the loudest voices.

Zebedee   Changes the power balance.

Tom   In favour of those with a degree in circus skills.

Jen   In favour of equality. Probably not much like where you came from, is it?

Tom   I'm not mocking –

Jen (*to* **Tom**, *making a fist*)   This is 'veto'. (*Holds up her two index fingers.*) This is 'direct response' – I want to reply directly to that point. (*Makes a 'T' with her hands.*) This is 'technical point', if you want to propose say breaking into smaller groups.

Tom   Smaller groups? There's only four of us.

Jen (*to the group*)   So we're still agreed on the trial?

Zebedee *and* **Joan** *show agreement.* **Tom** *does 'hands on an invisible glass wall'.*

Jen   Tom?

Tom   I don't even know what you're talking about.

They lean into a discussion.

Ray   Are we not having . . . you know, a thing, Kelly?

Kelly   We are having a 'thing', Ray, it's called sex.

Ray   Do we not have a thing more than just that thing?

Kelly   Are you getting romantic with me?

Ray   Why are you not supporting me then?

Kelly   OK. Right. Supporting you.

Ray   Backing me up.

Kelly   I like you, Ray. The last thing I expected when I came down here was a holiday romance with extra tear gas, but you're funny, you're charismatic, I'd even say in the highly unlikely event I wanted to be impregnated and Olivier Giroud wasn't returning my calls, I'd put you on my initial shortlist –

Ray *(blushing)*   Well now, Kelly, you don't need –

Kelly   But you are also a fuckwit.

Ray   I am not –

Kelly   You stomp about shouting and yelling and refusing to make any compromises whatsoever, totally contradicting the fact that what you really want, more than anything else, is to belong to a *group*. Don't you? *(Beat.)* And a group has to be *worked at*. Solidarity isn't born, it's built up, layer by layer, out of the tedious sediment of discussion.

Ray   I fucking hate meetings.

Kelly   Real democracy is boring, slow, probably the most inefficient way to achieve social progress – and, it's the thing that makes us different.

Ray   I won't do it, Kel. I'd rather go and chuck a Molotov.

Kelly   Anyone can chuck a Molotov. Only a genuine revolutionary can make it through an affinity group.

She gestures at the group. **Ray** *puts his hands on his hips and exhales heavily.*

Ray (*muttering*)   Fuck's sakes . . .

Kelly   Come on.

Beat, then the two of them join the circle.

Jen   Why won't anyone hold the bankers to account? Thirteen trillion in bailouts, six million people made homeless in the US alone, and has anyone been arrested? Has anyone even been fired?

Tom *holds up his index fingers.*

Zebedee   Quick learner.

Tom   Me.

Zebedee   Really?

Tom   Yeah. There's been a lot of layoffs, actually. We're not all Fred the Shred. Carry on.

Jen   So we decided to do it ourselves. Put it on trial: not just bankers, the whole system. First thing was to find a proper courtroom. I remembered this place.

Kelly   I've been past it out clubbing a hundred times and never knew it was here.

Zebedee   So we found a way in.

Joan   That was the fun part.

Kelly   Fixed up the toilets and the electrics.

Joan   Clambering up trees, over walls. I haven't done that since I was a little girl.

Kelly   It's in a lot better nick than when we arrived.

Jen   The council tried to have us chucked out so they could do, um, absolutely nothing with it, but we got a court stay in our favour.

Kelly   Which is why the police charged us out of the square. (*Points at* **Jen**'s *head.*) Can't let us get on top, can they?

Zebedee   We have a prosecutor –

He mock-bows and pulls out a sheaf of notes.

We have a defence lawyer –

At **Ray**, *who rolls his eyes.*

Zebedee   We even have a judge –

Joan   Real judge, retired, coming down from Wolverhampton. He sounds quite excited.

Tom   But no bankers? Nobody physically on trial?

Jen   No.

Zebedee   We invited them. They told us to fuck off.

Tom   But –

Zebedee   If you don't agree, you should do the disagreement gesture.

Tom   Right. What's the disagreement gesture?

The group do the disagreement gesture – hands wave, fingers down, palms inward.

Tom (*muttering*)   Fuck's sakes.

He does the disagreement gesture.

What's the point? You don't actually have them in the room, what's the point?

Kelly   Because it's not for them. They have their say all the time: it's called government policy. It's for the rest of us.

Ray   Everybody thinks austerity is necessary because we're told it is, over and over again. If enough people repeat a lie enough times, it becomes true. Boris Johnson is a harmless clown. John Terry is a legitimate member of the human race. Austerity is necessary.

Kelly   No one puts that idea on trial. They quibble at bits of it, but no one takes it on head-on, in a public forum.

Tom   A public forum of people like you?

Joan   We're not 'like us'. Like what others think we are. Shouty. Here to burn things down.

Ray   Speak for yerself, Joanie.

Joan   I do.

Kelly   A lot of people, maybe most people, have a very strong sense that things are wrong, but they don't know what's right. And nor do we. That's the point. That's what makes it exciting.

Tom   It sounds a little self-indulgent maybe.

Jen   Not if we take it seriously. That's why we voted for Ray as defence –

Ray   Nothing like elections to put you off democracy.

Jen   Because he's our most persuasive speaker. He's the guy we most want to believe. And so he's the one who has to express what we don't want to believe.

Tom *looks at* **Ray** *with an expression of 'That makes sense.'* **Ray** *shrugs grumpily.*

Tom   I still don't see what it's going to change.

Joan   My late husband used to say that life was a process of narrowing down, of casting people off, till you ended on a small dark island, alone.

Tom   Cheery fella.

Joan   I'd have divorced him if he hadn't died first. Always had to have the last word, the sod. Thing is, he proved himself

right. Because people do leave you. They die, or they retire to
Spain, same thing. He died because he was afraid, and because
it was the easiest thing to do. It was easier to give up and fade
away than make himself vulnerable to the possibility of
something better. And so he pulled his own coffin lid closed.
I won't do that. I'll keep my eyes open to the bitter end. (*Beat.*)
And with that, I don't half need a wee.

She gets up and heads to the toilet. A knock at the door.

Zebedee   'It's been a long time, I shouldn't have left you.'

Ryan (*off*)   'Without a strong rhyme to step to.'

Zebedee *opens the door.* **Ryan** *enters with several Starbucks in a
cardboard carrier.*

Ryan   Classic tune.

He touches fists with **Zebedee**.

Ryan   I dunno who likes cappuccino or latte so I got some
of each.

Zebedee *looks horrified.*

Ryan   What?

Zebedee   Starbucks!

Ryan   And?

Zebedee   Nobody in this movement drinks Starbucks!

Ryan   I spent my own fucking money on these!

The circle gets up and comes towards **Ryan**.

Jen   How much did you spend, Ryan?

Ryan   I dunno, tenner?

Jen   That's ten pounds more tax than Starbucks have paid in
the last three years.

Ryan   Where I'm from, Jen, this is all there is.

Ray (*reaching for a cup*)   It is actually quite cold in here, isn't it though? Actually?

Zebedee   Are you seriously gonna – ?

Ray (*offering* **Zebedee** *one*)   Actually quite cold actually?

Zebedee   I'd rather gargle with Michael Gove's urine. Thanks though.

Ray   Ah, go on, it can't be that – (*He takes a drink and spits it out.*) See if you can get your money back.

Ryan   Fuckin' will do.

Zebedee   There's a fair-trade place round the corner. Come on, I'll show you.

Ryan   Fucking fair-trade . . .

They leave. **Ray** *shuts the door.*

Jen   Do you wanna help out, Tom?

Tom   How? I'm not going on trial if that's what –

Kelly   You know the system. Challenge us.

Jen   Tell us when we get too fanciful.

Beat.

Tom   Look, I don't . . . At the risk of sounding like a patronising ex-banker: I don't know if you really understand what you're dealing with. I live in a block of flats in Bow, and from my balcony you can see the City, squatting like a spider atop the town, daring anyone to take it on. And when you're in there, that's how you feel: where the fuck else would you want to be? I did an internship before my last year at uni, I'd never given a thought to finance before, but when you walk in, you're just like, 'Holy fuck. I want to work here.' Miles and miles of chrome and glass and a billion flickering numbers that pile up around you like snowdrifts . . . And you can press a button and change the value of the currency in Argentina. Press another one and a thousand people in Mumbai lose their jobs. Do you have any idea how good that feels? How seductive it is to know that people know you can do that to them, and are afraid of you? And even when you don't understand one fucking word of what is going on, Exhibit A, the derivatives market, which is why we had the financial crisis and are going to have another one, the outside world doesn't know that. Or have any idea how to change it. Do you really think you're going to stop all that, change the real rulers of this country, the system that keeps politicians on their knees, with (*gestures round the room*) this?

Beat.

Kelly   I don't know.

Tom (*urgent*)   Well, why not? Because they will eat everything.

Jen   We know that.

Tom   They will never ever ever change, because that is the most well-oiled machine for the extraction of value since the Roman Empire, and if a part malfunctions or starts to play up (*raises his hand*) they will have it out before you can blink. Nothing personal. (*Beat.*) I came down here because I would very much like to feel my contribution to this life was something more than making money out of pain. But if you're going to raise our hopes that things can be different, you have to give us an alternative. (*Looking around.*) Don't you?

Kelly   All my mates ask me that. And when I tell them we don't have one, yet, they look all smug. Like I failed the test, so they're allowed to keep their shit facial hair and retro T-shirts and ironic hipster detachment that masks an abyss of emptiness. Like they don't have to think.

Tom   I'm not trying to be a dick. I just . . . I need this.

Kelly   Before I came here I was a student. Anthropology. In terms of making a living you'd be better off burning twenty grand's worth of scratchcards, but totally fascinating. One of the books we read was about debt. The writer was talking to this woman about the IMF and the horrible shit it gets up to, and after he laid out that people *die* in the name of austerity, have been doing in Africa for quite some time, she just looked at him and said: 'But they have debts. They have to pay them.' And he was amazed by this, that debt has such a powerful hold on us that a perfectly reasonable woman can think it's better for people to die than for financial imbalances to be corrected. And he started to dig into why. And he concludes, five hundred pages later, that it's because our deepest social ties and obligations – to our ancestors, to the society that birthed us – we express in terms of debts. That at its deepest level, debt is our word for love.

Tom   Hah. That's quite . . . I never thought of it like that.

Kelly   Debt is our word for love. And love is the thing we're most frightened of. And you can't take on a deep, atavistic, millennia-old thing like that without a new space and a new language. It's not the answers right now, it's the questions. We are trying to learn to ask the right questions, ones that don't start with money, that start with people. Asking those questions: that's the alternative, Tom.

Jen   And it's the action. The action of doing this, of *doing* something, not just moaning. Things change because people *do things*. Ideas come mainly from actions. It's *actions* that give people the sense things can be changed.

A knock at the door.

Ray   Some rap shit.

No answer. Another knock. They look at each other.

Jen   Ryan?

A third, more insistent knock. **Jen** *nods to* **Ray** *to open the door. It opens to reveal* **McDonald Moyo** *in hi-vis jacket, hard hat and clipboard.*

McDonald   Good afternoon. Health and Safety.

Jen *goes very still.* **Ray** *is amused.*

Ray   Health and Safety?! Em, I think you've the wrong place, fella.

McDonald (*checks his clipboard*)   I don't think so.

He steps inside and begins to take stock of the place, kicking a loose floorboard and making notes. **Ray** *goes to* **Jen** *with a wry expression. She looks worried.*

Ray   The fuck is this shite?

Jen   If we fail Health and Safety they can have us out within the hour.

Ray   You serious?

Jen   It's the quickest and least violent way to dispose of an occupation.

Ray   I cannot believe, as a revolutionary autonomist movement, that we have to abide by Health and Safety legislation.

Jen   Clever bastards.

She approaches **McDonald***.*

Jen   Hi, I'm Jen.

McDonald (*not stopping his work*)   Pleased to meet you.

Jen   Can I get you a cup of tea or anything?

McDonald   No thank you.

Beat.

Jen   You know we have the right to stay?

McDonald   That's nothing to do with me. I'm here to ensure your safety.

He moves around the room, taking notes. **Jen** *and* **Kelly** *look on with concern.*

Ray   It's like *Strictly*, is it?

McDonald   Excuse me?

Ray (*nods at clipboard*)   The notes. A few friendly suggestions on improving our style. How's my cha-cha? So to speak.

McDonald *pushes past him.* **Ray** *steps in his way.*

Ray   Would you see yerself more as Bruno or Darcey, I wonder, fella?

McDonald (*looks at him*)   Excuse me.

He gestures at the other side of the room. Beat. **Ray** *steps aside.*
McDonald *moves past him, taking more notes. Pause.*

Kelly   Listen, can we – ?

McDonald   You intend to use the venue for public gatherings?

Jen   Yes, we do.

McDonald   That adds to your responsibilities.

Kelly   How so?

McDonald   It brings into play workplace legislation. The Health and Safety at Work Act of 1974.

He kicks a loose floorboard.

Kelly   We've been –

McDonald   The Workplace (Health, Safety and Welfare) Regulations 1992 . . . (*He pulls down a wall panel.*) Dear oh dear, what kind of cowboy has done this?

Jen   Us.

Kelly   We're fixing up the place. To hold this trial.

McDonald   May I ask what qualifications you possess?

Kelly   We've made it loads nicer since we got –

McDonald   Construction qualifications.

Jen   We're building a new world, if that's any good to you.

Beat. **McDonald** *shakes his head and makes another note on the clipboard.* **Joan** *enters, wiping her hands on a rag.*

Joan   Toilets are still in a terrible state, I've been trying to – McDonald?

McDonald *stares at her and stiffens. Beat.*

McDonald   Hello.

Joan   It's me, Joan. Do you remember –

McDonald   I remember you. Yes. Hello.

Joan   You came to –

McDonald   You made me a cup of tea. Yes. Thank you. Now if you don't mind . . .

Joan *steps back, hurt.* **McDonald** *continues his work. They watch. Pause.*

Tom   Growth industry. Health and Safety.

Beat.

McDonald (*not looking at them*)   Is it?

Tom   It is, yeah. Health and Safety, prostitution and repossession.

Ray   There's a shocker.

McDonald (*looks up at* **Ray**)   Meaning?

Ray   The only way to make money these days is fucking people.

Jen   Helpful.

McDonald   Health and Safety is not fucking people. Health and Safety is helping people. It is duty of care and the protection of workers' lives. Not that people like you would know much about working.

Kelly   We've been fixing this place up for a week.

Jen   'People like you'?

McDonald   Excuse me?

Jen   'People like you', you said. What did they tell you?

McDonald   It was an expression.

Jen   The police, before you came in here. What did they tell you?

McDonald   Nobody told me anything. Just that it was an old building, and unsafe for –

Kelly   About us.

Beat. **McDonald** *flicks a look at* **Joan**. *He goes back to his work.*

Joan   McDonald –

McDonald   Please don't talk to me.

Joan   But –

McDonald   My first job, OK? This is my first job –

Joan   Just let us tell you why –

McDonald   Please, Joan.

A knock at the door.

Ryan/Zebedee (*off*)   'Think of how many weak shows you slept through – '

Ray *opens the door.* **Zebedee** *and* **Ryan** *come in with coffees, which they start to hand out.*

Ryan   'Time's up, sorry I kept you.' Got my money back from Starbucks.

Tom   How?

Ryan   Told 'em otherwise we'd occupy the shop.

Jen   Would you like a coffee?

McDonald   No, I . . .

Ryan   They even gave me some free muffins, look.

Ryan *is talking over his shoulder as he approaches* **McDonald**. *He throws out a couple of muffins, turns his head and they come face to face.* **Ryan** *drops a coffee.*

Kelly   Shit, I'm so sorry, let me…

She starts to clean up the spilled coffee. **Ryan** *is first to break away.*

Ryan (*to the group*)   Fucking come on then.

Ray   What?

Ryan   Fix up these fucking floors. Standing around like cunts. Come on!

He grabs a floorboard and a hammer and starts to beat it into place. **McDonald** *stares at him, icy cold. Beat. He turns calmly to the group.*

McDonald   As I was saying: the application of workplace legislation.

Ryan *bangs louder to try to drown him out.*

McDonald   The Provision and Use of Work Equipment Regulations 1998, the Management of Health and Safety at Work Regulations 1999, the Fire Safety Order of 2005 –

The floorboard splits. **Ryan** *holds the broken end in one hand. Beat.*

McDonald   And the adequate provision of toilets. Where are they, please?

A couple of hands point dumbly in the direction of the toilets. **McDonald** *marches off.* **Ryan** *throws the broken piece of wood viciously away.*

Zebedee   What the fuck is going on? Ryan? What –

Ryan   Don't fucking talk to me. Don't fucking talk to me, you hippy cunt.

He turns his back on them, distraught.

Kelly   Ryan, will you please tell us what's going on?

Ryan *doesn't look at them. Pause.*

Joan I'm going to get him a cup of tea.

Ray Oh, that should make all the fucking differ.

Joan He likes tea. I'm going to get him a tea.

*She stops by a distraught **Ryan** as she leaves and speaks quietly into his ear.*

Joan I don't know what you're afraid of, but I know what fear looks like. I was married to it most of my life. Don't give in.

*She leaves. The rest helpless. **Zebedee** kicks a plank in futile rage and sulks. Pause.*

Kelly All to waste.

Tom Where would you start?

Zebedee What's the fucking point?

Tom Because this will get done.

Kelly But not here. Not in the place that's perfect for it, in front of the media, of hundreds of people who might not come back if –

Tom But it will get done. Won't it? Or what are you doing here? If you can get knocked off course by a . . . (*Beat. Insistent.*) Where would you start?

Jen We're starting with debt.

Ray The debt they're always telling us we have to pay back. We don't.

Tom Course we do.

Kelly No, we don't. Tell him, Zeb.

Zebedee Oh, fuck off.

Kelly I'll do it then.

She grabs a piece of paper from his back pocket and reads from it.

'The "a government – '

Zebedee (*unsuccessfully grabbing for it back*)   Oy! That's my –

Kelly   We're a collective, aren't we?

(*Reads.*) 'The "a-government-is-like-a-family, it-has-to-balance-its-books" metaphor is a devious lie. Family debts are nothing like national debts. When times get tight – '

Zebedee   Yes, alright, alright. (*To* **Tom**.) When times get tight a government can print more currency. A family can't go up in the loft and bang out more money.

Ray   Unless your name is Harry Redknapp.

Zebedee   All an indebted government has to do to get out of trouble is make sure its debt grows more slowly than its tax base. The tax base grows, the debts fade away. It's what the Americans did after the Second World War.

Kelly   Which makes Osborne letting corporations off billions in tax, plus making people unemployed instead of taxpayers, even more insane.

Zebedee   But the main reason we don't have to pay these debts is they're not ours to pay. There's a thing called odious debt. Odious debt was legalised by the Americans after they stole Cuba from the Spanish. They didn't fancy paying Cuba's debts, so they cast around and found a fella called Alexander Nahum Sack. Sack had this doctrine of odious debt, which held that . . . Hang on…

He leans over **Kelly***'s shoulder to consult the notes.*

Ray   Spit it out son, as the priest said to the altar boy.

Kelly   Ray.

Tom   Yeah, but the international markets –

Zebedee (*holds up a hand*)   Held that if the debt was incurred for specific rather than national interests, and the lenders knew that, 'This debt is not an obligation for the nation; it is a *regime's* debt, a personal debt of the power that incurred it.

The creditors have committed a hostile act with regard to the people.'

Jen   Sound like anywhere you know?

Zebedee   'Legally, the debts of the State must be incurred for the needs and in the interests of the people.'

Kelly   That *doesn't* sound like anywhere I know.

Zebedee   If the bank bailout was used for the benefit of a tiny clique at the expense of ordinary people, we don't have to pay it back.

Tom   Bollocks.

Zebedee   It's quite clear under international law. The UN Charter states that full employment and social and economic welfare take precedence over all other obligations, including debt repayments. The UN Human Rights Council states that 'The exercise of the basic rights of the people of debtor countries to food, housing, clothing, employment, education and health cannot be subordinated to economic reforms arising from debt.'

Tom   Yeah, but international law is largely hortatory, isn't it?

Ray   It's what?

Tom   It's there for encouragement. It's not binding.

Ray   I'll use that next time. 'Well, officer, I wasn't going to smash the bank windows in, but then I remembered that the law is largely hortatory.'

Zebedee   The principle of *force majeure* allows for cancellation of international debt on grounds of financial necessity. Under the internationally established principle of the State of Necessity, quote, 'a State cannot be expected to close its schools and universities and courts, to disband its police force and to neglect its public services to such an extent as to expose its community to chaos and anarchy, merely to provide the wherewithal to meet its moneylenders, foreign or national'.

Jen 'No democratic government can bear the long-lasting austerity exacted by international institutions.' Henry Kissinger, would you believe.

Zebedee (*scribbling the quote down*)   Where'd you get that one?

Jen   Wikipedia.

Zebedee *stops writing and grimaces.*

Jen   Ah go on, fuck it, no one'll know the difference.

Tom   If you tried that in any serious way, the markets would rip you apart. A run on the currency, bond spreads go up, cost of borrowing through the roof –

Ray   Not necessarily. I give you the case of Ecuador.

Tom   Give me the case of Ecuador.

Ray   So the Ecuadorians took a squizz round and thought, 'Funny, all this "aid" all these years and the president is covered in gold leaf and we've one spare pair of undies for the entire country,' and decided to carry out a debt audit. They came to the conclusion that seventy per cent of the debt had disappeared up a fat man's nose, and they wrote it off. They offered their creditors thirty cents in the dollar. What's that they say on the pension adverts? 'The value of your investment may go down as well as up.'

Zebedee   And ninety-five per cent of the creditors took it. Because that's how you deal with markets. You bully them. You do not let them bully you.

Kelly   In Mesopotamia, three thousand years ago, they held a Debt Jubilee every seven years. The clay tablets recording the debts were publicly smashed and the slate wiped clean. Because even the Mesopotamian equivalents of George Osborne had enough sense to realise that the repression of an ever growing percentage of the population can't, in the long run, be sustained. And out of self-interest if nothing else, they let the debt go.

Jen   There's a beautiful thing happening right now called the Rolling Jubilee. People are pooling money, buying up poor people's debt for pennies on the dollar, and abolishing it. Just poof! Letting it go, getting their fellow citizens out from under the thumb. Look it up online.

Pause.

Tom   Why don't I know all this stuff?

Ray   The point of an Oxford education, old boy, is not 'to learn', it's 'not to learn'.

Tom   I was at Cambridge.

Jen   You know it now.

Tom   But if all that's true . . .

Jen   Yes?

Tom   And we don't have to pay this money back?

Jen   Yes?

Tom   Then why are we doing it?

Jen   Oh, well that one's easy.

Ray (*making his fingers into guns*)   Stick 'em up! It's a robbery!

Zebedee   Austerity doesn't 'work' because it's not supposed to 'work'. Or rather, it's not supposed to fix things. What it is supposed to do, and this it's doing rather well, is to transfer an overwhelming amount of money and power to a tiny elite. It's a coup, mate. It's the same thing they did to Russia, to Latin America, the same thing the World Bank's been doing to Africa for decades and calling it 'development'. It's a *heist*: the greatest heist in the history of the modern world.

Pause.

Jen   You see the alternative now? (*Taps her head.*) Starts up here.

Kelly (*to* **Jen**)   I see how you do it now.

Tom   But . . . you have such an obvious agenda, it makes it hard to –

Ray   An agenda?! Of course we have an agenda. Everybody's got an agenda. You think *The King's Speech* didn't have an agenda? 'How tough it is to be the king. Aaaah. Kings are people too.' Fuck off. If it's so fucking hard to be the king, I've an idea for you: r-r-r-r-r-resign. a-a-a-a-a-abdicate. And while you're at it, d-d-d-d-d-dissolve the fucking monarchy, ya cunt.

Tom   It was a shit film.

Ray   *Downton* fucking *Abbey*: 'Wouldn't it be nice if we all went back to the nineteenth century, when men were men and poor people were raped in the scullery?' There's nothing without an agenda, Tommy.

Jen   That is where they wanna take us, Tom. Back to the Victorians: an aristo elite giving charity to the deserving poor and incarceration to the undeserving poor. The basic project of the people in charge of this country is to undo the twentieth century, and we are not going to let them do that. We are going to fight them, brick by brick and bone by bone.

McDonald *enters, writing on his clipboard. He looks over his notes. Turns over a page. And another. And another. And another, for effect. There's a lot of notes.*

McDonald   Well. Thank you for your co-operation.

He starts to move towards the door. A knock. He stops.

Joan (*off*)   'It's been a long time, I shouldn't have left you. Without a strong rhyme to step to.'

Ray *opens the door, giggling a bit despite the situation.*

Ray   You're a one, aren't you Joan?

Joan   There is a code. I used the code. (*Hands* **McDonald** *a cup of tea.*) Tea.

McDonald   I don't want –

Joan   Two sugars.

Beat. He takes the tea. She gestures at **Ryan**.

Joan   We'll leave you to it.

McDonald   I don't –

She shrugs at him, gestures to the group and they slip away, leaving **McDonald** *and* **Ryan**. *Pause.*

Ryan   You're waiting for my apology.

McDonald   I don't give a fuck what you say.

Ryan   You do though. Or you'd be gone.

They make eye contact for the first time.

It's not just me, you know. Lot of people have put a lot of work into this.

McDonald   So what?

Ryan   You can't punish them for what I did.

McDonald   I can do whatever I want. I can do *whatever* I want.

Ryan   Then go. Door's open.

Beat. He nods towards where the group has gone.

They're alright, these.

McDonald   I don't care.

Ryan   They're brave. They stand up and say, 'This is what I want.' I've never said that to anyone.

McDonald   You want me to feel *sorry* – ?!

Ryan   It makes you vulnerable. Gives people something to hurt you with. We'd do anything not to be hurt, most of us. (*Beat.*) I am sorry for what I did to you.

McDonald   If that is your apology, I do not accept it.

Ryan   That's up to you.

McDonald   In any form I do not accept it.

Ryan   Up to you. (*Beat.*) This is what I want: I want this thing to go ahead. Please.

McDonald *pulls back his shirt to reveal a colostomy bag. Beat.*

Ryan   Is that permanent?

McDonald   They don't know. (*Beat.*) Do you know how much work I lost? This is my first job and now you, *you* of all people want me to . . . My child was barred from school because –

He shoves **Ryan** *aside and makes for the door.* **Ryan** *grabs him.*

Ryan   Just listen, please.

McDonald   No! Why should I? Who listened to me, who cared for me all those nights in the hospital, all those mornings in the freezing rain clearing up other people's shit and puke and blood? Why should I care about this godforsaken country when it has never, for one moment, cared for me? (*Beat.*) *Why?*

Ryan   You don't know these people.

McDonald   What do they know?

Ryan   Why don't you ask them?

McDonald   What do they know about life? About suffering?

Ryan   Is it a competition? What's the prize?

McDonald   Every day now I look over my shoulder. I sweat and I shudder in crowds. I look at everyone, every man, every white man, as an enemy, because of you. You have ruined this country for me. You have narrowed my world.

Ryan   I'm sorry.

McDonald   I do not accept it.

Ryan   Then let me give you something else.

McDonald   Ccch! I won't take your money.

Ryan   The chance to do to me what I did to you.

Beat. **McDonald** *stares at him.*

McDonald   I don't carry a knife.

Ryan   I'm on probation. Anything kicks off, I'm back to bang up. You can say I assaulted you, abused you, whatever, they'll believe it.

McDonald *moves away.* **Ryan** *grabs his arm.*

Ryan   Alright. Listen. *Please.* If you shut this place down, where do you think I go?

McDonald   I don't *care* –

Ryan   You know where I go. You've been there.

McDonald   Where you belong.

Ryan   Where I belong. Yes. The people I know. The things I know how to do. What you said: a narrow world. If I go back to that pub, I am never coming out. If there isn't something else, if I can't *imagine* something else whether it's this or something different but the *possibility* of something else, I am never coming out. I'm asking you, one man to another, not to send me back there. (*Beat.*) There it is. I'm in your hands, mate.

Long pause.

McDonald   What is it you want to do?

Ryan   A trial.

McDonald   A trial?

Ryan   Yeah. (*Beat.*) Can I tell you about it?

Beat. **McDonald** *sips his tea. The others creep tentatively into the room.*

Lights slowly down.

Blackout.